HEART WATCHERS' COMPLETE DIET & MENU PLANNER

By Sylvan Lewis, M.D.

Frederick Fell Publishers
Hollywood, Florida

Library of Congress Cataloging-in-Publication Data

International Standard Book Number: 0-8119-0719-8
Library of Congress Catalog Card Number:

For Information Address:

Fell Publishing, Inc.
2131 Hollywood Boulevard
Hollywood, Florida 33020

Published simultaneously by Prentice-Hall Canada, Inc.

Manufactured in the United States of America
1 2 3 4 5 6 7 8 9 0

Table of Contents

Acknowledgment

Virginia Aronson, R.D., M.S. is a registered dietician with a master's degree in nutrition. She is the author/co-author of ten books, including *The White House Family Cookbook* with Executive Chef Henry Haller (Random House, 1988).

Ms. Aronson assisted in the development of the Heart Watchers' Diet Plan, and was responsible for the selection and testing of all recipes included herein. She has helped to ensure that the *Heart Watchers' Complete Diet & Menu Planner* is both nutritious and delicious.

DIET
AND
YOUR HEART

Risking It

Approximately one million Americans die each year and many millions more are disabled due to heart attacks and coronary artery disease. Cardiovascular disease is currently America's number one health problem. Yet, there are definite preventative measures that you can take to increase your odds against this killing, crippling threat.

Blood cholesterol, blood pressure and body weight are three major factors that influence the overall health of the heart and cardiovascular system. Most people today are aware of the importance of these health components, yet many do not understand how diet can control these factors and their subsequent effects on cardiovascular health.

Use the following simplified *Self-Test* to determine just how well your present lifestyle promotes your cardiovascular health. Indicate by (x) the most appropriate response to the following statements. Be honest!

Heart Watchers' Self Test

Yes   No   Unsure

——— ——— ———— 1. I have a family history of high blood pressure, heart disease, circulatory disorders, and/or stroke.

——— ——— ———— 2. I have diabetes.

——— ——— ———— 3. I smoke cigarettes.

——— ——— ———— 4. I do not exercise regularly.

——— ——— ———— 5. I am often tense and feel stressed.

——— ——— ———— 6. I have a high blood cholesterol level (over 200).

——— ——— ———— 7. I have high blood pressure (above 140/90).

——— ——— ———— 8. I am overweight.

If you answered "no" to all of these statements, your risk of developing cardiovascular disease is probably quite small. Your lifestyle is "Heart Healthy!" However, the more "yes" responses you gave, the more risky your lifestyle is, and the more chances for potential heart problems are increased.

This *Self-Test* actually illustrates the eight major "risk factors" which are believed to contribute to the development of cardiovascular disease. By controlling these risk factors, it may be possible for you to reduce your chances of ever having a heart attack, circulatory disease or stroke. The eight risk factors are:

- family history of cardiovascular disease
- diabetes
- cigarette smoking
- physical exercise

- stress
- high blood level of cholesterol or other fat-like substances (hyperlipidemia)
- high blood pressure (hypertension)
- overweight

Your susceptibility to cardiovascular disease is actually partially determined before you are born by your individual genetic make-up; if you have a history in your family of cardiovascular disease and/or diabetes, your chances of developing these disorders are greater. Diabetics are more prone to cardiovascular diseases. Control over the other six risk factors, however, is basically a matter of education and self-responsibility — once you learn how you can support the health of your heart and cardiovascular system, it then becomes your responsibility to do so. Note also that the risk factors are additive, making the elimination of each risk factor a healthy step toward total cardiovascular well-being.

"Heart Watchers' Complete Diet & Menu Planner" can assist you in controlling the three diet-related risk factors: blood cholesterol level, blood pressure and overweight. Simply by following the *Heart Watchers' Diet Plan*, you may help decrease your blood cholesterol level, lower your blood pressure and rid yourself of excess weight all at the same time! Why risk the possibility of developing ill health, when you can be "Heart Healthy?"

But What Does It All Mean?

If you have a basic understanding of the relationship between diet and overall health, you can make the necessary dietary improvements. Yet, how much do you really know about the role of diet in cardiovascular health? Use the *Heart Watchers' IQ Quiz* to determine this by reflecting on the following questions and answering them as honestly as possible:

Heart Watchers' IQ Quiz

Yes　No　Unsure

_____ _____ _____ 1. Do you understand what your blood cholesterol level reflects and its impact on overall health?

_____ _____ _____ 2. Can you identify foods high in fat and cholesterol?

_____ _____ _____ 3. Do you understand the relationship between being sodium (salt) and cardiovascular health?

_____ _____ _____ 4. Can you identify foods high in sodium?

_____ _____ _____ 5. Do you understand the relationship between being overweight and overall health?

_____ _____ _____ 6. Can you identify foods high in fat and calories?

If you can honestly answer "yes" to all of these questions, then you probably have a basic understanding of cholesterol, sodium, fat, and calories, and the specific roles they play in your diet and in cardiovascular disease. Your next step is to utilize this knowledge to improve your diet and overall health.

If, however, you answered "no" to one or more of these questions, a lack of nutritional knowledge may be interfering with your ability to adopt a true *Heart Watchers'*

Diet. Rather than continue in ignorance and postpone possible health improvements that accompany dietary change, why not learn about diet and cardiovascular disease before you try to control them?

First, Cholesterol

Cholesterol is a waxy, fat-like substance that is made in the body by the liver, and is also provided through dietary intake. The level of cholesterol in your blood is determined both by the amount your body produces, and by the quantity you consume: the consumption of certain dietary fats, "saturated fats," also stimulate cholesterol production.

Cholesterol is important for a variety of body functions and is a normal portion of the blood and tissues. In recent years, blood cholesterol levels have been used to predict the chances for heart attack, circulatory disorders and stroke. This is because the amount of cholesterol in the blood is an accurate reflection of the degree of atherosclerosis, the disease primarily responsible for heart attacks, circulatory disorders and strokes.

Atherosclerosis is the process by which fatty materials, including cholesterol, are deposited in the lining of the arteries. These deposits build up and increase in size, narrowing the arterial opening. If the artery that supplies blood to the heart is blocked, the result is a heart attack. If an artery that supplies blood to the extremities is blocked, circulatory disorders and claudication can result. And, if the artery feeding the brain is blocked, a stroke can occur.

Tables that give the "normal" levels for blood cholesterol set this range at 150-200. These are actually average values for Americans. The normal values for other populations where cardiovascular disease is rare, range from 130-140! Thus, a blood cholesterol level of 200 may be considered normal, but it is actually only an average, and may be, in reality, quite unhealthy. The healthier range is below 200.

By changing your diet, you can help to lower your blood levels of cholesterol and other fatty substances to the below average, health-promoting levels. A low-cholesterol, low-fat diet may actually help to decrease your blood cholesterol level as much as 15 to 20 percent! The *Heart Watchers' Diet Plan* is designed to assist you in lowering blood cholesterol levels by modifying your intake of both cholesterol and saturated fats.

The following foods are high in cholesterol:

animal fats	egg yolks	milk, whole
bacon	eggnog	noodles, egg
beef, fatty cuts	hot dogs	pate de foie gras
beef, corned	goose	rabbit
brains	gravies	roe
butter	hamburgers	salt pork
caviar	heart	sausages
cheese, whole milk	ice cream	spare ribs
cold cuts	kidney	sweetbreads
cream, half & half	lamb fatty cuts	tongue
cream cheese	lard	tripe
cream, sour	liver	veal, fatty cuts
cream, whipped	luncheon meats	yogurt, whole milk

Note that only animal products contain cholesterol. Plant foods do not contain any cholesterol! Most of the above foods are not included in the *Heart Watchers' Diet*

Plan, and low-cholesterol substitutions are made for them. An occasional high-cholesterol, nutrient-rich food has been included, however, to enhance nutrient variety and promote diet adherence.

The following foods are especially high in saturated fats:

bacon	doughnuts
butter	fast foods
cheese, unless part-skim	fried foods
or skim	gravies
chicken fat	ice cream
chocolate, coca butter	lard
cream, half & half	margarine, unless diet
cream, sour	mayonnaise, unless diet
creamer, non-dairy	milk, whole
(made with coconut oil)	palm oil
cream cheese	pastries
croissants	peanut butter, commercial
coconut, coconut oil	yogurt, whole milk

Note that saturated fats are high in animal products that are also rich in fat. The only two vegetable oils that are saturated are coconut and palm oils. Most of the above foods are not included in the *Heart Watchers' Diet Plan,* and are replaced by low-fat substitutes. An occasional high-fat food will be allowed to enhance diet variety and acceptability.

By adhering carefully to the low-cholesterol (and low-*saturated* fat) *Complete 30-Day Heart Watchers' Menu Plan,* you can work toward lowering your blood cholesterol levels while enjoying nutritious, delicious meals. And, continuing on the *Heart Watchers' Diet Plan* after the initial 30 days, can help you to further promote total cardiovascular health for a lifetime!

Second, Sodium

Sodium is a mineral important for proper body function and is naturally present in most foods in varying amounts. Sodium in also found in table salt (40 percent sodium), various seasonings, and as a common food additive. Sodium is added to certain medicinals, and is even present in water supplies. Obviously, we cannot totally avoid sodium -- nor would we want to. However, Americans tend to consume 10 to 20 times the amount the body requires.

High blood pressure is the most common cardiovascular disorder affecting Americans today, and a high sodium intake may contribute to its development in susceptible individuals. Sodium restrictions have been shown to be effective in lowering elevated blood pressure. Therefore, everyone should moderate sodium intake in order to decrease elevated blood pressure (especially ifyou have it), and possibly prevent its onset (if you are predisposed). Why risk worsening or developing cardiovascular disease when a few dietary changes can minimize the risk?

The typical American consumes between 10 and 20 grams of sodium in their daily diet, whereas the recommended amount is 1 to 2 grams. In order to moderate your intake of sodium, utilize the following suggestions:

- Remove the salt shaker from the table.
- Do not use salt or high sodium seasonings in cooking.
- Choose fresh foods rather than processed foods which often contain added sodium.

- Be careful in purchasing costly, low-sodium, "dietetic" foods, since the non-dietetic counterpart may not be excessively high in sodium (e.g. low-sodium bread, jelly).
- Salt substitutes can result in mineral imbalances and should only be used if prescribed by your physician.

The following foods are especially high in sodium:

anchovies
bacon
barbecue sauce
beans, lima
beef, corned
biscuits
bouillon
canned meat, fish,
    vegetables
caviar
cheese foods
chili sauce
chips
cold cuts
cooking wines
crackers, salted
dips
dried meats
frozen dinners
ham
hash browns
herring
horseradish
hot dogs
instant gravies
instant sauces

kosher meats
luncheon meats
meat extracts
meat sauces
meat tenderizer
nuts (unless unsalted)
pate de fois gras
peanut butter, commercial
peas, frozen
pickles
pickled meats, fish
pickled vegetables
pizza
popcorn, commercial
pot pies
relishes
roe
rolls, hard, submarine
salad dressing, commercial
salt--celery, garlic,
    onion, sea
salt pork
sardines
sauerkraut
sausages
seasoned pasta, rice

seeds (unless unsalted)	soy sauce
smoked meats, fish	tomato juice
stews, canned	vegetable juice cocktail
soups	worchestershire sauce

Read food labels carefully to identify those products which contain sodium in the form of:

- salt (sodium chloride)
- baking soda (sodium bicarbonate)
- sodium silico
- brine (salt & water)
- monosodium glutamate
- sodium sulfite
- di-sodium phosphate
- sodium saccharin
- sodium alginate
- sodium aluminate
- sodium benzoate
- sodium hydroxide
- sodium propionate

Most of the above foods and sodium compounds are not included or are minimized in the *Heart Watchers' Diet Plan*. Occasionally, a high-sodium, nutrient-rich food will be allowed to enhance variety and promote diet adherence.

And Third, Calories

Excess body weight is not only unattractive, but it is a health hazard as well. Overweight people are more likely develop:

- diabetes
- respiratory problems
- gallbladder disease
- infertility/difficult pregnancies

Overweight is also associated with an increased incidence of high blood pressure, heart disease, and other cardiovascular disorders. With more than one-third of the American population currently overweight, it is no wonder that cardiovascular disease is our number one health problem!

The *Heart Watchers' Diet Plan* is low enough in calories to allow for safe weight loss. The *Diet Plan* has a moderate caloric content, yet provides essential nutrients -- if followed properly. Do not deviate from the *Heart Watchers' Diet Plan* as outlined, and do not make substitutions in the *Heart Watchers' Menu Plan*. If you alter the *Diet* or *Menu* plans, you may not be obtaining all of the nutritive ingredients necessary for proper body functioning. This can lead to:

- irritability
- depression
- nervousness
- headache
- weakness
- dizziness
- fatigue
- other symptoms of caloric-nutrient deficiencies

And, if you make changes in the *Heart Watchers' Diet* or *Menu Plans,* you may not be successful in decreasing your cholesterol level, lowering your blood pressure, or losing excess weight. Instead, you might:

- feel deprived from the elimination of certain necessary foods.
- mistakenly substitute high-cholesterol, high-fat, sodium-rich, and/or high-calorie foods.
- alter the dietary balance.
- discontinue the *Heart Watchers' Diet* altogether.
- fail to improve both your diet and your health.
- fail to lose weight, an maybe even gain some weight!

Calories are a unit of measure, an amount of heat, used to express the energy provided by food. If a food is high in calories, it provides a lot of energy. If a food is low in calories, then it provides little energy. Your body needs a certain amount of energy each day in order to function properly. If you take in too much energy (too many calories), the extra will be stored as body fat. If you do not take in enough food energy to meet your needs (too few calories), then you will lose body fat. This balance can be expressed in a simple formula:

- Excess calories = too much energy = stored body fat = weight gain
- Inadequate calories = use of body fat for energy = weight loss

It is the latter balance that the *Heart Watchers' Diet Plan* can help you to achieve. All you have to do is follow the *Diet and Menu Plan,* -- carefully and accurately. While the caloric intake may be low, your nutritional status will not suffer. In fact, it should improve!

The key number to remember is 3,500: there are 3,500 calories in one pound of body fat. In order to **gain** one pound of body fat, you must take in 3,500 calories **more** than your body needs. and in order to **lose** one pound of body fat, you must take in 3,500 calories **less** than your body requires.

You need not try to create a 3,500 calorie deficit in a single day. Instead, spread out your total calorie decrease and subsequent weight loss over several days, a week, a month or a year. If you lower your caloric intake by 500 calories a day, you should lose one pound in a week (500 x 7 = 3,500, or one pound). This can result in a four to five pound weight loss in a single month (one pound/week x four to five weeks = four to five pounds). And, after a year, the total weight loss will be more than 50 pounds (one pound/week x 52 weeks = 52 pounds)!

These weight loss estimates are of actual body **fat**. With the *Heart Watchers' Diet Plan,* you will also lose excess body **fluids** that are retained on high-sodium diets. Since body fluids weigh as much as body fat, weight loss may be more than the amounts indicated above. Remember, the *Heart Watchers' Diet and Menu Plans* should be followed carefully. The *Plans* are designed to allow for loss of body fat, and loss of accumulated body fluids, without creating any nutritional deficiencies.

Weigh yourself once a week **only**, in the morning, without clothing. Each week, record your weight and compare it to the *Desired Weight Chart* on page 116. By charting your weight, you are also able to visualize your weekly rate of weight loss.

There is no need to try to hasten your weight loss rate. The *Heart Watchers' Diet Plan* allows for a sensible, regular loss of excess weight, safely and effectively, while at the same time contributing to lower blood cholesterol levels, decreased blood pressure, and improved overall health.

Why risk poor heart health, when simple, preventive measures can result in improved cardiovascular condition and a longer, healthier life? You can start today, with the *Heart Watchers' Diet Plan.*

The Importance of Exercise

On a low-calorie diet plan, the body uses its own **fat** stores to supply necessary energy. However, unless regular exercise is incorporated into the daily regimen, the body will also burn its own lean **muscle** tissue for energy. Thus, it is essential for good health and good looks (who wants those baggy arms and extra folds following weight loss?) to include sustained physical activity on a daily basis.

The best kinds of activities for weight loss and heart health are **aerobic exercises**. To further your weight loss efforts, help reduce blood cholesterol and blood pressure, and enhance self- esteem and self-image, adopt an aerobic exercise plan:

- Exercise at least three times a week for at least 20 minutes.
- Select activities that make you "huff and puff," such as brisk walking, jogging, bicycling and aerobic dancing.
- Start slowly, don't overdo, and learn to enjoy the time you are devoting to yourself and your health.

Note: *It is wise to check with your physician before embarking on an exercise program, especially if you are over the age of 40, overweight, and/or suffering from ill health.*

New Scientific Discovery

Recent research has revealed a remarkable nutritional discovery: eating certain types of fish may play a role in the prevention of heart disease! Studies have shown that a special chemical component found in fatty fish may help to reduce blood pressure and the blood clogging associated with heart disease risk. Nutritionists now recommend the inclusion of two or three servings of seafood each week. The following choices are especially rich in the heart-healthy "omega-3 fatty acids:"

anchovies	rockfish
bass	sablefish
bluefish	salmon
hake	sea trout
halibut	smelt
herring	swordfish
lake trout	tuna (fresh)
mackerel	Also: eel
mullet	muscles
ocean perch	oysters
pollock	scallops
pompano	squid
rainbow trout	other fish and seafood in lesser amounts

The **Heart Watchers' Diet Plan** includes fish and seafood several times a week, not only as low-fat, low-calorie substitutes for meat, but to ensure an adequate intake of heart- healthy fish oils as well.

Note: Don't fall for advertising claims that promote fish oil/omega-3 supplements! Research has not shown that such supplements provide healthful assistance, and ingestion of fatty acids in large doses may actually prove to be harmful to your health!

Another New Nutritional Discovery

New research indicates that **mono**unsaturated fats -- not **poly**unsaturated fats, not **saturated** fats -- may be helpful in reducing the risk of heart disease. Populations with diets emphasizing foods rich in monosaturated fats demonstrate lower incidences of cardiovascular diseases. Thus, nutritionists now recommend the substitution of monounsaturated food choices for polyunsaturated and saturated fats. Of course, it is essential for weight loss to keep your **total** fat intake low.

The following items are especially rich in monounsaturated fats:

> avocado
> olive oil
> peanut oil

In order to increase the monounsaturated fat content of your diet, the *Heart Watchers' Menu Plan* includes avocados in moderate amounts, and substitutes olive and peanut oils for other vegetable oils and fats, where appropriate.

More New Nutritional Findings

Nutrition is a relatively new science, and researchers are discovering more and more diet and health information every year. In the area of preventative medicine, the role of certain nutrients in protecting the body against disease is slowly unraveling. New studies have pinpointed possible preventative functions of potassium, calcium and magnesium for hypertension, and fiber for high blood cholesterol. A well-balanced diet includes adequate amounts of these three essential minerals and plenty of fiber-rich foods. The **Heart Watchers' Diet Plan** emphasizes mineral-rich and high-fiber foods.

Note: *It is unnecessary to rely on nutritional supplements for obtaining adequate amounts of essential minerals. In fact, large doses of certain minerals can be toxic! Special fiber supplements are also unnecessary, unless prescribed by your physician to treat a specific disorder.*

HEART WATCHERS' DIET PLAN

The *Heart Watchers' Diet Plan* is a complete guide to low- cholesterol, low-sodium, low-calorie eating. It is nutritionally balanced, and includes a wide variety of delicious, health-promoting foods. Simply by following the Complete *30-Day Heart Watchers' Menu Plan*, you can properly alter your diet, an important step toward improved cardiovascular health.

The *Heart Watchers' Diet Plan* is carefully designed so that each day, your total intake of:

- **cholesterol** is no more than the recommended 300 milligrams.
- **sodium** is no more than the recommended 1,000 to 2,000 milligrams.
- **calories** is within the safe fat-loss range of 1,200 to 1,500.

Also, the **Heart Watchers' Menu Plan** has been specially constructed to ensure that your total intake of:
- **fat** is low, emphasizing the **mono**unsaturated choices.
- **fish** is generous to emphasize rich sources of omega-3 fatty acids.
- **minerals** and **fiber** is adequate to take advantage of the possible role in heart health.

To speed up weight loss and the reduction of blood cholesterol and blood pressure, add **aerobic exercise** to your new lifestyle pattern. Your body will thank you for it!

Start now: simply follow the *Complete 30-Day Heart Watchers' Menu Plan.* It has been designed to fit the *Heart Watchers' Diet Plan,* so be sure to adhere to the *Menu Plan* carefully and accurately. Deviations and substitutions could adversely affect your dietary goals. Remember to use the *Easy Shopping Planner,* to guide you in purchasing and stocking the appropriate foods for your weekly *Heart Watchers' Diet Plan.*

Once the initial 30 days are over, you should be familiar enough with low-cholesterol, low-sodium, low-calorie eating that you can plan your own menus. Use the *Planning Counter* on pages 99-113 to assist you. And, when dining out, follow the suggestions outlined in the *Dining Out Do's and Don'ts* on pages 95-98 to help you make appropriate food selections.

The "Heart Watchers' Complete Diet and Menu Planner" can help you to better understand the importance of diet in cardiovascular health. With the proper knowledge, you can accept the responsibility required for you to make dietary changes. Your diet can become an important step in the road to improved cardiovascular

health, and a supportive structure in the path to overall
health and well-being.

Complete 30-Day Heart Watchers' Menu Plan

Note: In following the *Menu Plan,* be sure to read all
labels carefully to ensure that:
- fruit juices are unsweetened
- canned fruits are packed in juice, not syrup
- crackers are unsalted
- low-calorie dressings are low in fat and contain no
  more than 10 calories per teaspoon
- cheese is "Weight Watchers'," "Life-Line," or other
  low-calorie brand; mozzarella is "part-skim"

Also Note:
- Tea can be lightened with skim mild or enlivened
  with fresh lemon.
- Decaffeinated coffee can be substituted for herb tea.
- Use of diet margarine is optional when indicated.
- Plain low-fat yogurt is best, but flavored yogurt can
  be substituted when indicated.
- Use of old-fashioned "health-food" style peanut
  butter instead of commercial brands.
- Use the recipe for *Egg Substitute* to replace eggs in
  baking, if desired.
- Use the recipe for *Tomato Sauce* in place of commer-
  cial sauce, if desired.
- Drink plenty of water between meals to quench

thirst and aid in digestion.

(*The italicized menu items have recipes included on pages 39-81.)

KEY: Tbsp. = tablespoon   sm. = small
        tsp. = teaspoon   med. = medium
        oz.   = ounce   sl. = slice

Day One

Breakfast:	4 oz. orange juice
	2/3 cup *Low-Fat Granola* with
	    1/3 cup skim milk and 1/2
	    small banana, sliced

Lunch:	*Lite Spinach Salad* with 1 tbsp. *Ranch-Style Dressing* 3-4 whole grain crackers 1 small apple
Dinner:	4 oz. *Herbed Fish* 1/2 cup brown rich 1/2 cup steamed broccoli tossed salad with 1 Tbsp. *Zero Dressing*
Snack:	2-3 gingersnaps *Club Soda Cooler*

Day Two

Breakfast:	4 oz. grapefruit juice
	1 cup bran cereal with
	    1 cup skim milk and
	    1/2 cup sliced strawberries

Lunch: *Ratatouille* with assorted raw
             vegetables and 2-3 whole-
             wheat bread sticks
             1 small fresh peach
Dinner: 3 oz. *Lemon Chicken*
             1 small red potato, baked with
                1 Tbsp. *Mock Sour Cream*
             1/2 cup steamed green beans
             tossed salad with 1-2 tsp.
                low-calorie dressing
             8 oz. skim milk
Snack: 3 cups hot-air popcorn
             club soda or spring water

Day Three

Breakfast: 4 oz. pineapple juice
             1 cup *Swiss Muesli*
             Herb tea
Lunch: *Turkey Salad*
             3-4 whole grain crackers
             1 medium orange
Dinner: *Spaghetti 'n Broccoli*
             tossed salad with 1-2 tsp.
                low-calorie dressing
             1 slice Italian bread with 1 tsp.
                diet margarine (if desired)
Snack: 8 oz. skim milk

Day Four

Breakfast: 1/2 medium grapefruit
             1 *Low-Fat Bran Muffin*
             8 oz. skim milk

Lunch: *Chef's Lite Salad* with
              1-2 tsp. low-calorie dressing
          1 small whole grain roll
          1 small fresh pepper
Dinner: 3-4 oz. *Steamed Fish*
          1/2 cup brown rich
          1/2 cup steamed baby carrots
          tossed salad with 1/2 Tbsp.
              low-calorie dressing
          1/2 cup seedless grapes
Snack: 2-3 graham crackers
          1 cup low-fat vanilla yogurt

Day Five

Breakfast: 4 oz. orange juice
            Fruit Crunch Muffin
            Herb tea
Lunch: 1/2 cup *Spinach Dip* with
                assorted raw vegetables and
                3-4 whole-grain crackers
            2 medium plums
Dinner: 3 oz. extra lean hamburger
                patty on 1 small whole-grain
                roll with 1 slice low-fat
                cheese and lettuce,
                shredded, and 1-2 slices
                fresh tomato
            1 small apple
Snack: *Yogurt Sipper*

Day Six

Breakfast:	4 oz. grapefruit juice
	Bubbly Fruit Broil
	Herb tea
Lunch:	*Peanut Butter 'n Banana Sandwich*
	8 oz. skim milk
	1 small nectarine
Dinner:	1 1/2 cups *Chinese Vegetables* on
	1/2 cup brown rice
	tossed salad with 1-2 Tbsp.
	low-calorie dressing
	1 cup *Fruited Yogurt*
Snack:	3 cups hot-air popcorn
	club soda or spring water

Day Seven

Breakfast:	4 oz. apple juice
	1 *Whole Wheat Waffle* with
	1/2 cup sliced strawberries
	and 1 Tbsp. *Mock Sour Cream*
Lunch:	1/2 cup *Hummus* with 1 small
	whole wheat pita, in wedges
	1 cup low-fat yogurt
	(lemon, if desired)
Dinner:	*Curried Shrimp Salad*
	1/2 cup steamed pea pods
	1 small whole grain roll with
	1 tsp. diet margarine (if desired)
	1/2 cup sliced papaya
Snack:	*Cracker Melt*
	Club soda or spring water

Day Eight

Breakfast:	4 oz. orange juice
	2/3 cup *Low-Fat Granola* with
	1/3 cup skim milk and
	1 small banana, sliced
Lunch:	*Heart Healthy Salad* with
	1 Tbsp. *Lite Cheese Dressing*
	3-4 whole grain crackers
	1 small apple
Dinner:	1 cup *Chili*
	tossed salad with 1 Tbsp.
	Avocado-Lite Dressing
	1 *Whole Grain Corn Muffin* with
	1 tsp. diet margarine (if desired)
	8 oz. skim milk
Snack:	1 cup fresh fruit salad
	club soda or spring water

Day Nine

Breakfast:	4 oz. grapefruit juice
	1 cup bran cereal with
	1/2 cup skim milk and
	1/2 cup sliced strawberries
Lunch:	*Gazpacho* with assorted raw
	vegetables and 2-3 whole
	wheat bread sticks
	1 sm. fresh peach
Dinner:	*Vegetable Rice Casserole*
	tossed salad with 1-2 tsp.
	low-calorie dressing
	8 oz. skim milk
Snack:	*Yogurt Sipper*
	2 fig cookies

Day Ten

Breakfast:	4 oz. pineapple juice
	1 cup *Swiss Muesli*
	Herb tea
Lunch:	*Salmon Pasta Salad*
	3-4 whole-grain crackers
	1 med. orange
Dinner:	*Bean Tortillas* (2)
	tossed salad with 1 Tbsp.
	Avocado-lite Dressing
	1 cup low-fat yogurt (vanilla or
	lemon, if desired)
Snack:	assorted raw vegetables
	club soda or spring water

Day Eleven

Breakfast:	1/2 med. grapefruit
	1 *Whole Wheat Blueberry Muffin*
	with 1 tsp diet margarine
	(if desired)
	Herb tea
Lunch:	*Chef's Lite Salad* with 1-2 tsp.
	low-calorie dressing
	1 sm. whole grain roll
	1 sm. fresh pear
Dinner:	*Tuna Broiler*
	3-4 slices fresh tomato
	1/2 cup steamed asparagus
	8 oz. skim milk
Snack:	1 cup fresh fruit salad with 1 cup
	low-fat yogurt (vanilla or
	lemon, if desired)

Day Twelve

Breakfast:	4 oz. orange juice *Fruit Crunch Muffin* Herb tea
Lunch:	1 cup *Spiced Cheese Dip* with assorted raw vegetables and 3-4 whole grain crackers 1 sm. apple
Dinner:	*Stuffed Pepper* tossed salad with 1 Tbsp. *Italian-lite Dressing* 1/2 cup fruit *Sorbet* with sliced fresh fruit
Snack:	2 fig cookies 8 oz. skim milk

Day Thirteen

Breakfast:	4 oz. grapefruit juice *Bubbly Fruit Broil* Herb tea
Lunch:	*Peanut Butter 'n Date Sandwich* 8 oz. skim milk 1 sm. nectarine
Dinner:	*Black Beans 'n Rice* tossed salad with 1 Tbsp. *Avocado-lite Dressing* 1 cup cubed mangos
Snack:	1 cup *Fruited Yogurt*

Day Fourteen

Breakfast:	4 oz. apple juice
	2 *Whole Wheat Pancakes* with
	1/2 cup fresh blueberries and
	1 Tbsp. *Mock Sour Cream*
Lunch:	1 cup *Cucumber Dip* with
	assorted raw vegetables
	1 sm. whole grain roll with
	1 tsp. diet margarine (if desired)
Dinner:	*Chicken Cacciatore*
	1/2 cup brown rice
	tossed salad with 1 Tbsp.
	Italian-Lite Dressing
	1 sm. wedge honeydew melon
Snack:	*Slim Shake*

Day Fifteen

Breakfast:	4 oz. orange juice
	2/3 cup *Low-fat Granola* with
	1/3 cup skim milk and
	1/2 cup sliced strawberries
Lunch:	*Heart Healthy Salad* with
	1 Tbsp. *Lite Cheese Dressing*
	3-4 whole grain crackers
	1 sm. banana
Dinner:	*Scallop K-bobs*
	1 ear fresh corn-on-the-cob with
	1 tsp. diet margarine (if desired)
	tossed salad with 1 tbsp.
	low-calorie dressing
	1 sm. apple
Snack:	*Yogurt Sipper*

Day Sixteen

Breakfast:	4 oz. grapefruit juice
	3/4 cup oatmeal with 1/4 cup
	skim milk and 1 Tbsp. raisins
Lunch:	*Gazpacho* with assorted raw
	vegetables and 2-3 whole
	wheat bread sticks
	1 sm. fresh peach
Dinner:	*Turkey Parmagiana*
	tossed salad with 1 Tbsp.
	Italian-Lite Dressing
	1/2 sm. sweet potato, baked, with
	1 tsp. diet margarine (if desired)
	1-2 figs
Snack:	*Yogurt Crumble*

Day Seventeen

Breakfast:	4 oz. pineapple juice
	1 cup *Swiss Muesli*
	Herb tea
Lunch:	1 cup *Marinated Broccoli*
	3-4 whole grain crackers
	1 med. orange
	1 cup low-fat yogurt (vanilla
	or lemon, if desired)
Dinner:	3-4 oz. *Broiled Fillets With Mustard*
	1/2 cup wild rice
	1/2 cup steamed carrots
	tossed salad, with 1-2 tsp.
	low-calorie dressing
	1/2 cup seedless grapes
Snack:	3 cups hot-air popcorn
	Club Soda Cooler

Day Eighteen

Breakfast: 1/2 med. grapefruit
Cinnamon Toasties
8 oz. skim milk

Lunch: *Chef's Lite Salad* with 1 Tbsp.
Ranch-style Dressing
1 sm. whole grain roll
1 sm. fresh pear

Dinner: *Whole Wheat Pizza-ettes*
tossed salad with 1 Tbsp.
Italian-Lite Dressing
1 cup fresh fruit salad

Snack: 5-6 *Cucumber Rounds*
Club soda or spring water

Day Nineteen

Breakfast: 4 oz. orange juice
Fruit Crunch Muffin
8 oz. skim milk

Lunch: 1 cup *Veggie Dip* with assorted
raw vegetables and 3-4
whole grain crackers
1 sm. apple

Dinner: 3 oz. *Sherried Chicken*
1 sm. baked potato with 1 Tbsp.
Mock Sour Cream
1/2 cup steamed spinach with
lemon tossed salad with
1-2 tsp. low-calorie dressing
1 fig cookie

Snack: *Yogurt Sipper*

Day Twenty

Breakfast:	4 oz. grapefruit juice
	Bubbly Fruit Broil
	Herb tea
Lunch:	*Vegetable Tuna Sandwich*
	8 oz. skim milk
	1 sm. nectarine
Dinner:	*Spaghetti 'n Broccoli*
	tossed salad with 1 Tbsp.
	Italian-lite Dressing
	1 sl. Italian bread with 1 tsp.
	diet margarine (if desired)
	1/2 cup seedless grapes
Snack:	1 cup low-fat yogurt (vanilla or
	lemon, if desired)

Day Twenty-One

Breakfast:	4 oz. grape juice
	2 sl. *Apple-cinnamon French Toast*
	with 1/2 fresh strawberries
	and 1 Tbsp. *Mock Sour Cream*
Lunch:	1/2 cup *Mock Guacamole* with
	assorted raw vegetables and
	1 sm. corn tortilla, toasted, in
	wedges
	1 cup low-fat yogurt (vanilla or
	lemon, if desired)
Dinner:	3-4 oz. *Herbed Fish*
	1/2 cup steamed zucchini
	1 sm. red potato, baked, with
	1 tsp. diet margarine (if desired)
	tossed salad with 1 tbsp.
	Lite Cheese Dressing

       1/2 cup cubed mangos
Snack: *Slim Shake*

Day Twenty-Two

Breakfast: 4 oz. orange juice
       1 cup bran cereal with 1/2 cup
        skim milk and 3 sm. banana
Lunch: *Heart Healthy Salad* with
        1 Tbsp. *Zero Dressing*
       1-2 whole wheat bread sticks
       1-2 rings fresh pineapple
Dinner: *Bagel Pizza*
       tossed salad with 1-2 tsp.
        low-calorie dressing
       1/2 cup applesauce
Snack: *Cracker Melt*
       Club soda or spring water

Day Twenty-Three

Breakfast: 4 oz. grapefruit juice
       3/4 cup oatmeal with 1/4 cup
        skim milk and 1 Tbsp. raisins
Lunch: *Lite Spinach Salad* with
        1 Tbsp. *Ranch Style Dressing*
       3-4 whole grain crackers
       1 fig cookie
       8 oz. skim milk
Dinner: 1 1/2 *Chinese Vegetables* on
        1/2 cup brown rice
       tossed salad with 1-2 tsp.
        low-calorie dressing
       1 sm. pear
Snack: *Fruit "Sundae"*

Day Twenty-Four

Breakfast: 4 oz. pineapple juice
1 cup *Swiss Muesli*
Herb tea

Lunch: *Lite Carrot Salad*
1-2 whole wheat bread sticks
Peach Crisp
8 oz. skim milk

Dinner: *Creole Chicken*
1/2 cup brown rice
tossed salad with
1 Tbsp. *Italian-lite Dressing*
2 med. plums

Snack: 3 cups hot-air popcorn with
1 tsp. grated parmesan cheese
Club soda or spring water

Day Twenty-Five

Breakfast: 1/2 med. grapefruit
2/3 cup *Low-fat Granola* with
1/3 cup skim milk and
1/2 sm. banana, sliced

Lunch: *Ratatouille* with assorted raw
vegetables
2-3 whole grain crackers
1 sm. fresh peach

Dinner: 3 oz. lean lamb
1/2 *Cheese-stuffed Potato*
1/2 cup steamed asparagus with
lemon
1/2 cup steamed cherry tomatoes
tossed salad with 1 tsp.

low-calorie dressing
Snack: *Yogurt Crumble*

Day Twenty-Six

Breakfast: 4 oz. orange juice
                Fruit Crunch Muffin
                8 oz. skim milk and
Lunch: 1 cup *Marinated Vegetables*
                1 sm. whole grain roll
                1 med. tangerine
                1 cup low-fat yogurt (vanilla or
                    lemon, if desired)
Dinner: 3-4 oz. *Steamed Fish*
                1/2 cup wild rice
                1/2 cup steamed *Brussels sprouts*
                tossed salad with 1-2 tsp.
                    low-calorie dressing
                1/2 cup pineapple chunks
Snack: 3 cups hot-air popcorn
                Club Soda Cooler

Day Twenty-Seven

Breakfast: 4 oz. grapefruit juice
                Bubbly Fruit Broil
                Herb tea
Lunch: *Tuna Broiler*
                8 oz. skim milk
                1 sm. apple
Dinner: *Black Beans 'n Rice*
                tossed salad with
                    1 Tbsp. *Avocado-lite Dressing*
                1 cup cubed mangos

Snack:
1 cup low-fat yogurt (vanilla or
lemon, if desired)
5-6 *Cucumber Rounds*
Club soda or spring water

Day Twenty-Eight

Breakfast: 4 oz. orange juice
2/3 cup *Low-fat Granola* with
1/3 cup skim milk and
1/2 sm. banana, sliced

Lunch: *Cold Pasta Salad*
1-2 whole wheat bread sticks
1/2 cup *Sorbet*, with sliced fresh fruit

Dinner: 3 oz. baked turkey (no skin)
1/2 cup *Whole Wheat Stuffing*
1/4 cup natural cranberry sauce
1/2 sm. sweet potato, baked
tossed salad with 1-2 tsp.
low-calorie dressing
8 oz. skim milk

Snack: 1 cup *Fruited Yogurt*

Day Twenty-Nine

Breakfast: 4 oz. Apple Juice
1 whole wheat bagel, toasted, with
1 tsp. peanut butter
8 oz. skim milk

Lunch: *Vegetable-tuna Sandwich*
assorted raw vegetables
1 sm. peach

Dinner: *Polenta*
1/2 cup steamed kale with lemon

1/2 cup stewed tomatoes
tossed salad with 1 Tbsp.
Lite Cheese Dressing
1 cup fresh fruit salad

Snack: *Yogurt Sipper*

Day Thirty

Breakfast:
1/2 med. grapefruit
1 poached egg on
1/2 whole wheat English muffin
Herb tea

Lunch:
1/2 cup *Hummus* with 1 sm. whole
    wheat pita, in wedges
1 cup low-fat yogurt
    (lemon, if desired)
1 sm. apple

Dinner:
3-4 oz. broiled swordfish
    with lemon
1/2 cup *Bulgar-wheat Pilaf*
1/2 cup steamed broccoli
1/2 cup steamed summer squash
tossed salad with
    1 Tbsp. *Zero Dressing*
1/2 cup blueberries

Snack:
2 graham crackers
8 oz. skim milk

HEART WATCHERS' RECIPES

Breakfast Dishes

Low-Fat Granola

4 cups rolled oats
1 cup wheat germ
2 Tbsp. unprocessed
    bran
1/4 cup chopped walnuts
1/4 cup slivered almonds
2 Tbsp. sesame seeds

2 Tbsp. raisins
2 Tbsp. chopped dates
1/4 cup honey
1/4 cup vegetable oil
1/2 cup water
1-2 tsp. diet margarine

1. In a large bowl, mix together oats, wheat germ, bran, nuts and seeds.
2. Stir in dried fruit.
3. In a small saucepan, combine honey, oil and water; heat over low heat until just warm.
4. Pour warm liquid over dry ingredients and stir until well mixed.
5. Grease two baking sheets with diet margarine; spread out granola evenly.
6. Bake at 225 degrees for 1 1/2 to 2 hours, or until golden brown and crisp; turn cereal using a spatula every 15 minutes to brown evenly.
7. Store in an airtight container in the refrigerator.
   Yields about 8 cups

Swiss Muesli

1 cup commercial family cereal	*2 Tbsp. raisins*
	1 Tbsp. honey
1 small apple, cored and diced	*1 cup vanilla low-fat yogurt*

1. In a mixing bowl, combine cereal with fruit.
2. Add honey and yogurt, stirring until well mixed.

Serves 2

Low-Fat Bran Muffins

1/4 cup diet margarine	*1 cup unprocessed bran*
2 Tbsp. honey	*1/4 cup wheat germ*
2/3 cup skim milk	*1 Tbsp. baking powder*
1 egg	*1/4 tsp. salt*
1/4 cup molasses	*12 dates, chopped*
1 cup whole wheat flour	

1. In a mixing bowl, cream margarine with honey.
2. Blend in milk, egg and molasses.
3. In a separate bowl, combine flour, bran, wheat germ, baking powder and salt.
4. Stir dry ingredients into liquid ingredients, mixing just enough to moisten.
5. Stir in dates. Do not overmix!
6. Fill paper-lined muffin tins 1/2 full.
7. Bake at 400 degrees for 12 to 15 minutes, or until toothpick inserted in center comes out clean.

Yields 15 muffins

Fruit Crunch Muffin

2 Tbsp. low-fat cottage
cheese
1 Tbsp. applesauce
1 Tbsp. raisins
1 Tbsp wheat germ

4 walnut halves, chopped
1/2 whole wheat English
muffin
dash of cinnamon
dash of nutmeg

1. In a small bowl, mix together cottage cheese, applesauce, raisins, wheat germ and nuts.
2. Spread onto muffin half and sprinkle with cinnamon and nutmeg.
3. Broil for 1 to 2 minutes, or until cheese is bubbly.

Serves 1

Bubbly Fruit Broil

1/4 cup low-fat cottage
cheese
1 Tbsp. crushed
pineapple

1 Tbsp. raisins
1 Tbsp. chopped dates
1/2 small cantaloupe
dash of cinnamon

1. In a small bowl, mix together cottage cheese, pineapple and dried fruit.
2. Scoop mixture onto center of melon half and sprinkle with cinnamon.
3. Broil for 1 to 2 minutes, or until cheese is bubbly.

Serves 1

Whole Wheat Waffles

1 1/4 cups whole wheat flour	1 egg yolk
1/4 cup wheat germ	1 1/2 cups skim milk
1 tsp. salt	3 Tbsp. vegetable oil
2 tsp. baking powder	2 Tbsp. honey
	3 egg whites

1. In a mixing bowl, stir together flour, wheat germ, salt and baking powder.
2. In a separate bowl, beat yolk with milk, oil and honey until well blended.
3. Stir liquid ingredients into dry ingredients until well mixed.
4. In a separate bowl, beat egg whites until stiff peaks form; fold into batter.
5. Pour into pre-heated, non-stick waffle iron and cook until golden brown.

Yields 10

Whole Wheat Blueberry Muffins

2 1/4 cups whole wheat flour	1 egg
1/4 cups unprocessed bran	1/3 cup honey
1 1/4 tsp. baking soda	1/4 cup vegetable oil
1/4 tsp. salt	1 3/4 cups buttermilk
	1 1/2 cups blueberries

1. In a mixing bowl, stir together flour, bran, baking soda and salt.
2. In a separate bowl, beat together egg, honey, oil and milk.
3. Stir in dry ingredients, mixing just enough to moisten.
4. Fold in blueberries. Do not overmix!

5. Fill paper-lined muffin tins 1/2 full.
6. Bake at 400 degrees for 15 to 20 minutes, or until toothpick inserted in center comes out clean.

Yields 12

Whole Wheat Pancakes

1 cup low-fat cottage
   cheese
1 egg + 1 egg white
1 cup buttermilk
2 tsp. honey

1 cup whole wheat flour
2 Tbsp. wheat germ
1 tsp. baking powder
1/2 tsp. baking soda

1. In a blender or food processor, blend cottage cheese with eggs, milk and honey.
2. In mixing bowl, stir together flour, wheat germ, baking powder and baking soda.
3. Add liquid ingredients, stirring just enough to moisten.
4. Cook on a hot griddle, turning each pancake once so that both sides are golden brown.

Yields 12

Cinnamon Toasties

2 whole wheat English
   muffins
2 tsp. diet margarine,
   melted

2 tsp. skim milk
2 Tbsp. honey
1/2 tsp. cinnamon

1. Split muffins in half and brush each half lightly with margarine.
2. Brush with milk, then honey. Sprinkle with cinnamon.
3. Toast at 350 degrees for 5 to 6 minutes, or until tops are crisp and browned.

Serves 2

Apple-Cinnamon French Toast

*1 egg + 1 egg white,
   beaten
1/4 cup skim milk
1/4 tsp. vanilla extract
4 slices whole wheat
   bread*

*1 cup applesauce
dash of cinnamon
dash of nutmeg
1 tsp. confectioners' sugar*

1. In a shallow bowl, mix eggs with milk and vanilla.
2. Cut each slice of bread in half on the diagonal.
3. Soak each slice in egg mixture for 3 minutes, turning once.
4. Heat a non-stick saute pan over medium heat; brown slices, turning once to brown evenly on both sides.
5. In a small saucepan, mix applesauce with cinnamon and nutmeg; warm over low heat.
6. Spread each slice of toast with around 1/4 cup of warm applesauce and sprinkle lightly with powdered sugar.

Serves 2

Lunch & Light Snacks

Lite Spinach Salad

1/3 lb. fresh spinach
4 large mushrooms,
sliced
1 scallion, chopped fine

1/4 cup sliced water chestnuts
2 eggs, hard-boiled
2 tsp. slivered almonds

1. Wash spinach well and dry thoroughly. Tear into bite-sized pieces.
2. In a small bowl, combine spinach, mushrooms, scallions and water chestnuts.
3. Separate cooked egg whites from yolks; discard yolks and sieve whites.
4. Sprinkle salad with egg white and almonds. Chill until serving.

Serves 1

Turkey Salad

3 oz. cooked turkey, diced
1 stalk celery, diced
2 Tbsp. crushed
pineapple

1/4 cup low-fat yogurt
lettuce leaf
sprig of fresh parsley

1. In a small bowl, mix turkey, celery and pineapple.
2. Stir in yogurt, mixing until well coated.
3. Arrange lettuce on serving dish. Top with mounded salad.
4. Garnish with parsley. Chill until serving.

Serves 1

Chef's Lite Salad

1 cup lettuce, in bite-
size pieces
1 med. tomato, in wedges
1/4 small green pepper,
sliced thin
1/4 cup shredded
red cabbage

2 small radishes, sliced thin
1 oz. cooked chicken or turkey
julienne
1 oz. low-fat cheese, julienne
1/4 cup sprouts

1. In a small bowl, toss lettuce with tomato, green peppers, cabbage and radishes.
2. Arrange strips of poultry and cheese across the top.
3. Spread sprouts across the top. Chill until serving.

Serves 1

Heart Healthy Salad

1 cup lettuce, in bite-
size pieces
1/4 medium carrot,
grated
1/2 small tomato, in
wedges
1/4 small green pepper,
sliced thin

1 stalk celery, diced
1/4 small cucumber, sliced
thin
1 Tbsp. sesame seeds
1 Tbsp. chopped walnuts
1 Tbsp. raisins
1/4 cup low-fat cheese
1/4 cup sprouts

1. In a small bowl, toss lettuce with carrot, tomato, green pepper, celery and cucumber.
2. Sprinkle with seeds, nuts and raisins.
3. Top with a scoop of low-fat cheese.
4. Spread top with sprouts. Chill until serving.

Serves 1

Curried Shrimp Salad

1/3 cup low-fat yogurt
1 tsp. curry powder
1/2 tsp. minced ginger
1 cup cooked shrimp

dash of freshly ground black
*   pepper*
lettuce leaf
sprig of fresh parsley

1. In a mixing bowl, combine yogurt with curry and ginger.
2. Add shrimp and pepper. Toss lightly.
3. Arrange lettuce on a serving dish. Top with a scoop of salad.
4. Garnish with parsley. Chill until serving.

Serves 1

Salmon Pasta Salad

4 oz. pasta shells, whole
*   wheat or vegetable*
1 small can (3 oz.)
*   salmon, drained*
1 Tbsp. chopped scallions
1/2 cup low-fat yogurt

1 Tbsp. buttermilk
1 tsp. lemon juice
1 tsp. dill
1 tsp. Dijon-style mustard
dash of freshly ground pepper
2 sprigs of fresh parsley

1. Cook pasta in boiling water for 7 minutes (al dente). Drain well.
2. In a mixing bowl, flake salmon. Stir in scallion and pasta shells.
3. In a small bowl, combine yogurt, milk, juice, dill, mustard and pepper.
4. Pour over salmon salad and toss lightly.
5. Cover with plastic wrap and chill for several hours before serving. Garnish with parsley.

Serves 2

Lite Carrot Salad

2 cups shredded carrots	2 Tbsp. lemon juice
1/2 cup raisins	2 lettuce leaves
1/4 cup diet mayonnaise	2 sprigs of fresh parsley
1/4 cup low-fat yogurt	

1. In a mixing bowl, combine carrots with raisins.
2. In a separate bowl, mix mayonnaise, yogurt and juice.
3. Pour over carrot salad and toss to coat evenly.
4. Chill for an hour or longer before serving.
5. Arrange lettuce on 2 serving dishes. Top each with a scoop of salad.
6. Garnish with parsley.

Serves 2

Cold Pasta Salad

1 cup broccoli florets	1/4 tsp. garlic powder
1/2 small red pepper, sliced thin	1 Tbsp. lemon juice
1 cup cooked pasta shells, whole wheat or vegetable	1 Tbsp. minced parsley
	dash of freshly ground black pepper
1 tsp. dry mustard	2 Tbsp. white wine vinegar
	1 Tbsp. olive oil

1. Steam broccoli and red peppers until tender crisp; cool.
2. In a salad bowl, mix steamed vegetables with pasta shells.
3. In a small bowl, combine mustard and garlic powder with lemon juice; stir in parsley and black pepper.
4. Whisk in vinegar; slowly whisk in oil until well blended.

5. Pour over pasta salad and toss. Chill for several hours.

Serves 2

Ratatouille

1 tsp. olive oil	1 cup diced zucchini
1 clove garlic, minced	1 cup eggplant cubes
1 Tbsp. chopped onions	1 tsp. oregano
1 small green pepper, diced	1 tsp. chopped parsley
1/2 cup tomato, diced	dash of freshly ground black pepper

1. Heat oil in a skillet and saute garlic and onion until golden.
2. Add green pepper, tomato and zucchini; saute for 3 minutes.
3. Add eggplant and saute for 2 to 3 minutes more, or until fork-tender.
4. Season with oregano, parsley and pepper. Transfer into a casserole dish.
5. Cover and bake at 350 degrees for 15 to 20 minutes, or until bubbling hot. Serve at once, or chill thoroughly and serve cold.

Serves 2

Spinach Dip

1 pkg. (10 oz.) frozen
     chopped spinach
1/2 cup low-fat cottage
     cheese
1 cup low-fat yogurt
3 Tbsp. diet mayonnaise

1/2 cup chopped parsley
2 Tbsp. chopped onion
1/2 tsp. dill
dash of freshly ground black
     pepper

1. Thaw spinach and drain well.
2. In a blender or food processor, puree cottage cheese to the consistency of sour cream.
3. In a mixing bowl, combine spinach with cottage cheese.
4. Stir in yogurt and mayonnaise, mixing well.
5. Add seasonings and mix well.
6. Chill overnight so that flavors can blend thoroughly.

Yields about 3 1/2 cups

Hummus

2 cups cooked garbanzo
     beans
1/4 cup sesame tabini

3-4 Tbsp. tamari
1-2 tsp. garlic powder

1. Cook beans until soft.
2. Mash beans in a blender or food processor.
3. Stir in tabini.
4. Add tamari and garlic to taste. Chill until serving.

Yields about 2 1/2 cups

Gazpacho

1/4 medium onion,
    chopped
1/2 medium cucumber,
    diced
1 cup tomato juice,
    low-sodium
1 clove garlic, minced

1 cup chicken broth,
    low-sodium
1 Tbsp. red wine vinegar
1 small jalapeno, diced
dash of freshly ground black
    pepper

1. In a blender or food processor, combine onion, cucumber, tomato juice and garlic; blend until smooth.
2. Add broth and vinegar; mix well.
3. Mix in jalapeno and black pepper. Chill for several hours before serving.

Serves 2

Spiced Cheese Dip

1 cup low-fat cottage
    cheese
3 Tbsp. low-fat yogurt
1 Tbsp. chopped chives

1 Tbsp. chopped parsley
1/4 tsp. thyme
dash of red pepper

1. In a blender or food processor, puree cottage cheese to the consistency of sour cream.
2. Add yogurt and blend well.
3. Add seasonings and mix well. Chill until serving.

Yields 1 1/2 cups

Cucumber Dip

1 large cucumber, peeled
* & seeded*
1 cup low-fat yogurt
2 tsp. lemon juice
1 clove garlic, minced

3 walnuts, minced
dash of low-sodium soy sauce
dash of freshly ground black
* pepper*

1. Grate cucumber and drain well.
2. In a small bowl, mix grated cucumber with yogurt and lemon juice.
3. Stir in garlic and nuts.
4. Season with soy sauce and pepper. Chill until serving.

Yields about 2 cups

Marinated Broccoli

3/4 cup cider vinegar
1 tsp. brown sugar
1 tsp. dill
1 tsp. freshly ground
* black pepper*

1/2 tsp. garlic powder
1 Tbsp. olive oil
2 cups broccoli spears

1. In a small bowl, whisk vinegar, sugar, dill, pepper and garlic.
2. Gradually add oil, shaking briskly.
3. Spread broccoli in a shallow dish. Pour on marinate.
4. Chill overnight. Drain before serving.

Yields about 2 cups

Cucumber Rounds

1 large cucumber, peeled
3/4 cup low-fat cottage
  cheese
2 tsp. minced onion

dash of garlic powder
dash of celery seed
dash of freshly ground black
  pepper

1. Slice cucumber into 1/2-inch thick rounds. Crisp in ice water for 1 hour.
2. In a small bowl, combine cottage cheese with seasonings. Chill.
3. Drain cucumbers and pat dry with paper toweling.
4. Arrange on serving dish and top each with a rounded tablespoon of the cottage cheese mixture.

Yields 10 to 12 rounds

Veggie Dip

2 cups low-fat cottage
  cheese
2 Tbsp. dill
1 Tbsp. chopped onion

2 Tsp. chopped parsley
dash of freshly ground black
  pepper
2 tsp. lemon juice

1. In a blender or food processor, puree cottage cheese to the consistency of sour cream.
2. Blend in seasonings and lemon juice.
3. Chill for several hours before serving.

Yields 2 cups

Mock Guacamole

1 can (15 oz.) garbanzo
    beans
1 Tbsp. olive oil
1/4 chopped onion
1 small clove garlic,
    pressed
1/3 cup chopped parsley

1/2 tsp. basil
1/8 tsp. salt
1/8 tsp. oregano
1/8 tsp. cumin
1/4 cup lemon juice
3 Tbsp. tabini

1. Drain beans and reserve 1/4 cup liquid.
2. In a blender or food processor, combine the liquid with oil, onion, garlic, parsley, basil, salt, oregano, cumin and lemon juice.
3. Blend until smooth.
4. Gradually add beans, blending well after each addition.
5. Blend in tabini. Chill until serving.

Yields 2 cups

Marinated Vegetables

1/2 cup sliced carrots
1/2 cup sliced celery
1/2 cup cauliflower
    florets
1/2 cup broccoli florets
1/2 medium onion,
    sliced thin

1/2 small green pepper, sliced
    thin
1/2 small zucchini, sliced thin
2-3 Tbsp. low-calorie Italian
    dressing or vinaigrette

1. Arrange vegetables in a shallow dish.
2. Add dressing and toss lightly, coating evenly.
3. Chill overnight. Drain before serving.

Yields 4 cups

Peanut Butter 'n Banana Sandwich

*2 slices whole wheat
    bread*
1 small banana

*2 tsp. old-fashioned peanut
    butter*

1. Spread 1 slice of bread with peanut butter.
2. Mash banana with a fork and spread on other slice of bread.
3. Fold together and slice in half diagonally.

Serves 1

Cracker Melt

4 rye crisps
1 tsp. Dijon-style mustard

1 slice low-fat cheese
1/4 cup sprouts

1. Spread crackers lightly with mustard.
2. Cut cheese into 4 squares and arrange on crackers.
3. Broil for 1 minute or until cheese is bubbly.
4. Top each with 1 tablespoon of sprouts.

Serves 1

Tuna Broiler

*1/2 cup water-packed
   tuna, drained*
1 Tbsp. chopped celery
1 Tbsp. chopped onion
*1 Tbsp. chopped green
   pepper*
1 Tbsp. chopped carrot

1 Tbsp. diet mayonnaise
dash of garlic powder
dash of freshly ground pepper
1 slice whole wheat bread
1 slice low-fat cheese
lettuce leaf

1. In a small bowl, flake tuna using a fork.
2. Stir in chopped vegetables and mayonnaise.
3. Season with garlic and pepper.
4. Spread evenly onto bread. Top with slice of cheese.
5. Broil for 1 to 2 minutes, or until cheese is bubbly.
6. Top with lettuce and sprouts.

Serves 1

Peanut Butter 'n Date Sandwich

*2 slices whole wheat
   bread*
2-3 dates, sliced thin

*2 tsp. old-fashioned peanut
   butter*

1. Spread 1 slice of whole wheat bread with peanut butter.
2. Arrange date slices evenly on the peanut butter.
3. Top with other bread slice. Slice in half diagonally.

Serves 1

Whole Wheat Pizza-ettes

1 small whole wheat pita
1/4 tsp. Dijon-style
* mustard*
4 slices fresh tomato
2 large mushrooms,
* sliced*

1 oz. part-skim mozzarella
* cheese*
dash of garlic powder
dash of freshly ground black
* pepper*
1 tsp. grated parmesan cheese

1. Cut pita into 4 wedges.
2. Spread each wedge with mustard.
3. Arrange tomato and mushroom slices evenly on wedges.
4. Cut mozzarella into 4 thin strips and arrange on top of the vegetables.
5. Season with garlic and pepper. Sprinkle with parmesan cheese.
6. Broil for 2-3 minutes or until cheese is bubbly.

Serves 1

Harry's Vegetable-Tuna Sandwich

1/2 cup water-packed
* tuna, drained*
1/4 small cucumber,
* chopped*
1/4 small zucchini,
* chopped*
2-3 small radishes,
* sliced thin*

2-3 cherry tomatoes, halved
1 Tbsp. low-calorie French
* dressing*
dash of freshly ground black
* pepper*
2 slices whole wheat bread
lettuce leaf
1/4 cup sprouts

1. In a small bowl, flake tuna using a fork.
2. Stir in cucumber, zucchini, radishes and tomato.
3. Add dressing and toss lightly to coat. Season with pepper.

4. Spread evenly on 1 slice of bread.
5. Top with lettuce leaf, sprouts and other bread slice. Serve in diagonal halves.

Serves 1

Bagel Pizza

    1 whole wheat or
       pumpernickel bagel
    2 Tbsp. tomato sauce
    1 oz. part-skim
       mozzarella cheese

    dash of garlic powder
    dash of freshly ground black
       pepper
    1 tsp. grated parmesan cheese

1. Slice bagel in half, and spread the top of each with 1 tablespoon of tomato sauce.
2. Slice mozzarella into 4 thin strips and arrange evenly on bagel halves.
3. Season with garlic and pepper. Sprinkle with parmesan cheese.
4. Broil for 2-3 minutes or until cheese is bubbly.

Serves 1

ENTREES

Spaghetti 'n Broccoli

1 head broccoli
1/2 lb. spaghetti, whole wheat
2 tsp. olive oil
1 Tbsp. minced garlic
4 medium tomatoes, chopped

1 cup tomato sauce
1 Tbsp. chopped basil
dash of freshly ground black pepper
dash of red pepper flakes
2 Tbsp. grated parmesan cheese

1. Cut broccoli into 1 to 2 inch pieces and separate florets. Steam until fork-tender.
2. Cook spaghetti in boiling water for 7 minutes (al dente); drain well.
3. In a large skillet, heat oil; saute garlic until golden.
4. Add tomatoes and saute for 1 minute more.
5. Stir in broccoli.
6. Add spaghetti, tomato sauce, basil and pepper. Bring to a boil.
7. Remove from heat; add grated cheese and toss lightly.

Serves 4

Chinese Vegetables

1 cup broccoli florets
1/2 cup green beans, in
    1-inch slices
1/2 medium onion,
    sliced thin
1/2 cup sliced mushrooms
1/4 cup shredded red
    cabbage

1/4 cup sliced water chestnuts
1/4 cup bamboo shoots
1/4 cup pea pods
2 Tbsp. low-sodium soy sauce
2 Tbsp. dry white wine
2 Tbsp. peanut oil
1 Tbsp. slivered almonds

1. In a large bowl, combine vegetables.
2. Add soy sauce and wine; toss lightly.
3. Heat oil in a skillet or wok.
4. Stir-fry vegetables until tender-crisp. Transfer to a serving dish.
5. Sprinkle with almonds.

Yields 3 cups

Vegetable-Rice Casserole

1 1/2 cups brown rice,
    uncooked
2 large tomatoes, sliced
    thin
1 medium zucchini, in
    1/2" slices
1 small eggplant, peeled
    & diced
1/2 cup whole wheat
    bread crumbs

1 egg + 2 egg whites, beaten
1 tsp. oregano
dash of freshly ground black
    pepper
3/4 lb. mushrooms, sliced
2 oz. part-skim mozzarella
    cheese
2 Tbsp. grated parmesan
    cheese

1. Cook rice. Spread evenly on the bottom of a 9 x 11-inch casserole dish.
2. Cover rice with a layer of tomato slices, then zucchini slices.

3. Steam eggplant until soft. Puree in a blender or food processor until smooth; blend in bread crumbs, eggs, oregano and pepper.
4. Spread evenly in the casserole dish.
5. Top with a layer of mushroom slices.
6. Slice mozzarella into thin strips and arrange evenly on casserole. Sprinkle with grated cheese.
7. Bake at 350 degrees for 45 minutes.

Serves 6

Bean Tortillas

1 1/2 cups kidney beans
1/2 cup chopped onion
1 cup chopped tomato
1/4 tsp. garlic powder
1 tsp. chili powder
dash of cayenne pepper
1 tsp. olive oil
1 clove garlic, minced
2 Tbsp. white wine
*   vinegar*

2 Tbsp. vegetable oil
1 tsp. low-sodium soy sauce
3 cups shredded lettuce
12 small corn tortillas
1/4 cup grated part-skim
*   mozzarella cheese*
1/4 cup grated parmesan
*   cheese*

1. Soak beans overnight in water; drain well.
2. In a saucepan, combine beans with onion, 1/4 cup of the chopped tomato, garlic powder, chili powder and cayenne.
3. Cook over medium heat until beans are soft.
4. In a small saute pan, heat olive oil; saute garlic until golden.
5. Mash garlic into beans, mixing well. Simmer for 10 minutes. Cover and remove from heat.
6. In a mixing bowl, stir together vegetable oil, vinegar and soy sauce.

7. Add lettuce and toss until well coated.
8. Bake tortillas until crisp.
9. Top each tortilla with 1/4 cup beans, 1/4 cup lettuce, 1 tsp. grated mozzarella and 1 tsp. grated parmesan. Serve with salsa.

Serves 6 (two each)

Black Beans 'n Rice

1 lb. black beans,
*   washed & drained*
2 bay leaves
1/4 tsp. freshly ground
*   black pepper*
1 Tbsp. olive oil

1 clove garlic, crushed
1/2 cup chopped onion
1 small green pepper, diced
4 cups cooked white rice

1. Cover beans with water and boil for 2 minutes. Cover pan and let stand for 1 hour.
2. Pour off water and replace with 6 cups fresh water.
3. Add bay leaves and black pepper. Bring to a boil.
4. Let simmer for 2 hours, adding water if needed.
5. In a small skillet, heat oil. Saute garlic and onion until golden.
6. Add green pepper and saute until tender-crisp.
7. Stir into beans. Serve over hot rice.

Serves 6

Polenta

6 cups water
2 cups cornmeal

1/4 cup diet margarine
4 oz. low-fat cheese

1. In a heavy saucepan, bring water to a boil.
2. Slowly add cornmeal, stirring consistently with a wooden spoon.

3. Add margarine, stirring until melted.
4. Cook over low heat for 2 to 3 minutes, stirring frequently, until smooth and thick.
5. Stir in cheese and let simmer for 1 minute more. Serve with tomato sauce, if desired.

Serves 4

Chili

1 lb. pinto beans	*2 cloves garlic, minced*
4 cups diced tomatoes	*2 tsp. oregano*
1 large jalepeno, diced	*1 tsp. chili powder*
1 medium onion, chopped	*dash of red pepper flakes*

1. Cook beans over low heat until soft.
2. In a mixing bowl, combine tomatoes, jalapeno, onion and garlic.
3. Add seasonings and mix well.
4. Stir in beans.

Serves 4

Herbed Fish

1 lb. firm-fleshed white fish (i.e. halibut)	*1/2 cup dry white wine*
1/8 tsp. basil	*1 Tbsp. lemon juice*
1/8 tsp. marjoram	*4 sprigs of fresh parsley*
1/4 tsp. chopped parsley	*4 slices fresh lemon*

1. Arrange fillets in a shallow casserole dish.
2. In a small bowl, stir together basil, marjoram and parsley.
3. Whisk in wine and lemon juice and mix well.
4. Pour over fish. Let marinate in the refrigerator for 1 to 2 hours.
5. Drain off marinade.
6. Bake at 400 degrees for 10 to 15 minutes, or until flaky.
7. Garnish with parsley sprigs and lemon juice.

Serves 4

Lemon Chicken

Juice of 2 lemons	*3 Tbsp. honey*
1 clove garlic, minced	*4 boneless chicken breasts skinned*
1 Tbsp. low-sodium soy sauce	*2 lemons, sliced thin*

1. In a small bowl, mix together lemon juice, garlic, soy sauce and honey.
2. Arrange chicken in a shallow casserole dish. Pour on marinade.
3. Let marinate in the refrigerator for at least 1 hour.
4. Bake at 325 degrees for 1 1/2 hours, basting frequently.
5. Garnish with lemon slices.

Serves 4

Steamed Fish

6-8 oz. fresh fish fillets
(e.g. salmon,
mackerel,
swordfish)
1-1 1/2 cups dry white
wine

1 tsp. fresh tarragon
dash of freshly ground black
pepper
2 sprigs of fresh parsley
2 slices fresh lemon

1. Arrange fillets in a saute pan.
2. Pour on wine to cover.
3. Sprinkle with tarragon and pepper.
4. Steam over high heat until flaky. Remove fillets and continue to simmer until liquid is reduced and thickened.
5. Pour over fillets and garnish with parsley and lemon.

Serves 2

Stuffed Peppers

1 1/4 cups tomato puree,
  low-sodium
1 small can tomato
  paste, low-sodium
1 Tbsp. oregano
1 1/2 tsp. basil
1 tsp. garlic powder
6 large green peppers
1 Tbsp. olive oil
1/2 medium onion,
  chopped
1/4 cup sliced mushrooms

2 Tbsp. chopped celery
1/2 lb. extra-lean ground beef
3/4 cup cooked brown rice
3 Tbsp. chopped walnuts
1 Tbsp. chopped parsley
1/4 tsp. thyme
1/4 cup chicken broth,
  low-sodium
3/4 cup low-fat yogurt
1 Tbsp. grated parmesan
  cheese

1. In a saucepan, combine tomato puree with tomato paste; stir in oregano, 1 teaspoon of the basil and garlic powder. Let simmer for one hour.
2. Slice tops off peppers; remove seeds and discard with tops.
3. Parboil peppers for 5 minutes.
4. In a large skillet, heat oil; saute onion until golden.
5. Add mushrooms and celery, and saute for 2 minutes or more.
6. Add beef and cook until browned. Drain off fat.
7. Stir in rice, nuts, parsley, thyme and milk. Mix well.
8. Stuff peppers with mixture and arrange in a deep casserole dish.
9. Add remaining 1/2 teaspoon of basil to chicken broth and stir into simmering tomato sauce. Bring just to a boil.
10. Pour sauce over and around stuffed peppers.
11. Cover and bake at 400 degrees for 45 minutes. Pepper should be tender.

12. Top each pepper with 1 tablespoon of yogurt and sprinkle each with 1 teaspoon of grated cheese.
13. Continue baking for 2 to 3 minutes or until yogurt melts.

Serves 6

Chicken Cacciatore

1 cup tomato sauce
1/2 cup sliced mushrooms
*1/2 cup chopped green
    pepper*
dash of oregano
*dash of freshly ground
    black pepper*

1 Tbsp. olive oil
1 small clove garlic, minced
*2-4 oz. boneless chicken
    breasts, skinned*

1. In a saucepan, mix tomato sauce with mushrooms, green pepper, oregano and black pepper.
2. Let simmer for 10 minutes.
3. In a skillet, heat oil; saute garlic until golden.
4. Add chicken; brown on both sides. Drain off fat.
5. Pour sauce over chicken and let simmer for 10 minutes, or until chicken is tender.

Serves 2

Scallop K-Bobs

*1 8 oz. can pineapple
    chunks*
1/4 cup lemon juice
*2 Tbsp. low-sodium soy
    sauce*
2 Tbsp. dry white wine

1 lb. bay scallops
12 large mushroom caps
12 cherry tomatoes
12 cubes of green pepper
2 tsp. olive oil

1. Drain juice from pineapple; reserve fruit.
2. In a small bowl, mix pineapple juice, lemon juice, soy sauce and wine.
3. Arrange scallops in a casserole dish and cover with marinade.
4. Let marinate in the refrigerator for 1 to 2 hours.
5. Drain liquid and reserve.
6. Thread scallops on skewers, alternating with mushroom caps, tomatoes, pepper cubes and pineapple chunks.
7. Brush with marinade then brush lightly with oil.
8. Broil for 8 to 10 minutes, or until scallops are tender; turn skewers once, and brush occasionally with marinade while cooking.

Serves 4

Turkey Parmagiana

2 Tbsp. whole wheat flour
dash of freshly ground black pepper
4 3 oz. turkey cutlets (boneless, skinned)
1 tsp. olive oil
1 clove garlic, crushed
1 Tbsp. chopped scallions
1/2 cup chicken broth, low-sodium
2 cups tomato sauce
2 oz. part-skim mozzarella cheese, shredded
1 Tbsp. grated parmesan cheese

1. In a shallow bowl, mix flour with pepper. Dredge cutlets.
2. In a saute pan, heat oil; saute garlic and onion until golden.
3. Add cutlets and saute until brown, turning once.
4. Transfer into a shallow casserole dish.

5. In a saucepan, combine broth with tomato sauce. Bring juice to a boil.
6. Pour sauce over cutlets and sprinkle with cheeses.
7. Bake at 350 degrees for 20 to 25 minutes or until hot and bubbly.

Serves 4

Broiled Fillets With Mustard

*1 pound fresh fish fillets
   (e.g. salmon,
   swordfish, bluefish)
1-2 Tbsp. Dijon-style
   mustard*

*1 tsp. olive oil
1/8 tsp. freshly ground black
   pepper
1 lime, cut in 4 wedges*

1. Arrange fillets on a baking sheet.
2. Brush lightly with oil.
3. Spread evenly with mustard. Sprinkle with pepper.
4. Broil for 7 to 10 minutes or until flaky and golden. Serve with a lime wedge.

Serves 4

Sherried Chicken

*2 large chicken breasts,
   halved and skinned
1/2 cup buttermilk
3 Tbsp. whole wheat
   flour*

*dash of rosemary
1 Tbsp. olive oil
1/3 cup dry sherry
4 sprigs of fresh parsley*

1. Dip chicken in buttermilk and dredge in flour. Sprinkle with rosemary.
2. Heat oil in a skillet; brown chicken on both sides, turning once.
3. Transfer chicken into a casserole dish. Bake at 425 degrees for 20 minutes.

4. Remove chicken; keep warm.
5. Simmer juices over medium heat. Add sherry, stirring constantly, and let simmer until thickened.
6. Pour sauce over chicken. Garnish with parsley.

Serves 4

Creole Chicken

1 1/2 lb. chicken, boneless and skinless
1/2 tsp. paprika
1 medium onion, sliced thin
1 small green pepper sliced thin

1/2 cup diced celery
1 can (16 oz.) whole tomatoes, low-sodium
1 can (16 oz.) whole mushrooms, low-sodium
dash of red pepper flakes
2 Tbsp. chopped parsley

1. Sprinkle chicken with paprika.
2. In a non-stick skillet, brown chicken on both sides.
3. Remove chicken from skillet; add onion, green pepper, celery, tomatoes and mushrooms. Bring to a boil, cover and let simmer for 10 minutes.
4. Slice chicken into bite-size pieces. Return to the skillet.
5. Add red pepper. Cover and let simmer for 40 minutes.
6. Sprinkle with parsley.

Serves 6

Beverages

Club Soda Coolers

> *3/4 cup club soda*   *1/4 cup grapefruit juice*
> *1/4 cup orange juice or*   *1 thick slice of fresh orange*

1. Pour club soda and juices into a tall, frosted glass.
2. Garnish with fruit.

Serves 1

Yogurt Sippers

> *3/4 cup low-fat yogurt*   *1 tsp. honey*
> *1/2 small banana and 2*   *crushed ice*
>   *dates or*
> *1/2 cup strawberries and*
>   *2 Tbsp. orange*
>   *juice*

1. In a blender, combine yogurt with fruit, honey and ice.
2. Blend until frothy.

Serves 1

Desserts

Fruited Yogurt

3 small bananas, sliced
3/4 cup seedless grapes
1/2 cup blueberries
1 medium orange, peeled
and sectioned

1 cup low-fat yogurt
1 tsp. vanilla extract
1 tsp. honey
1/4 cup orange juice

1. In a mixing bowl, combine fruit.
2. In a small bowl, mix yogurt, vanilla, honey and juice.
3. Stir yogurt into fruit and toss lightly. Chill for an hour or more before serving.

Yields 4 to 5 cups

Sorbet

2 cups fresh or frozen
fruit (strawberries,
raspberries,
blueberries, melon
balls, peaches or
sliced bananas)

2 Tbsp. confectioners' sugar
2 Tbsp. Kirsh
4 sprigs of fresh mint

1. In a blender or food processor, puree fruit with sugar and Kirsch to desired consistency.
2. Garnish with mint and serve with a side-dish of the appropriate fruit.

Serves 4

Betty's Yogurt Crumble

1/2 cup low-fat yogurt
1 small apple, grated
1 Tbsp. raisins

1 Tbsp. slivered almonds
2 graham cracker squares

1. In a small dessert dish, mix yogurt with fruit and nuts.
2. Crumble cookies over the top.

Serves 1

Fruit "Sundae"

1 cup strawberries
1/2 small banana, split lengthwise
1/3 cup low-fat cottage cheese
1 tsp. wheat germ

1 Tbsp. orange juice concentrate, defrosted but not diluted
1 Tbsp. chopped walnuts
1 Tbsp raisins

1. Place berries in the center of a shallow dessert dish.
2. Place banana slices on either side.
3. Top with a scoop of cottage cheese.
4. Pour on juice; sprinkle with wheat germ, nuts and raisins.

Serves 1

Peach Crisp

2 cups sliced peaches   *dash of cinnamon*
1 cup Grape Nuts cereal   *dash of nutmeg*
1/4 cup raisins   *1/4 cup vanilla low-fat yogurt*

1. In a small casserole dish, combine peaches with cereal.
2. Stir in raising; sprinkle with cinnamon and nutmeg
3. Cover and bake at 350 degrees for 15 minutes, or until steaming hot.
4. Serve warm, topped with a dollop of yogurt.

Serves 4

Dressings & Sauces

Ranch-Style Dressing

1/2 cup low-fat yogurt
1/2 cup diet mayonnaise
1/2 cup buttermilk
1 Tbsp. chopped parsley
1 tsp. chopped chives
1/8 tsp. freshly ground black
 pepper
1/8 tsp. red pepper
dash of garlic powder
dash of onion powder

1. In a blender, combine all ingredients
2. Blend until smooth. Chill until serving.

Yields 1 1/2 cups

Zero Dressing

1 cup low-fat cottage
 cheese
1/3 cup buttermilk
1/4 tsp. dry mustard
1 Tbsp. minced onion
1 Tbsp. chopped parsley
1 Tbsp. chopped chives
1 tsp. dill
dash of freshly ground black
 pepper

1. In a blender, combine all ingredients.
2. Blend until smooth. Chill until serving.

Yields 1 1/3 cups.

Lite Cheese Dressing

1/3 cup diet mayonnaise
1/4 cup lemon juice
2 Tbsp. grated
*   parmesan cheese*

1/4 cup cold water
dash of garlic powder
dash of freshly ground black
*   pepper*

1. In a covered jar, combine all ingredients.
2. Shake well.

Yields 1 cup

Avocado-Lite Dressing

1 ripe avocado, pitted
*   and peeled*
1 cup low-fat yogurt
1 Tbsp. white wine
*   vinegar*

2 Tbsp. skim milk
dash of garlic powder
dash of onion powder
dash of freshly ground pepper

1. Mash avocado until smooth.
2. Combine with remaining ingredients in a blender.
3. Blend until smooth. Chill until serving.

Yields about 1 1/2 cups

Italian-Lite Dressing

3/4 cup dry red wine
1 tsp. olive oil
1 tsp. red wine vinegar
1 tsp. oregano

1/8 tsp. freshly ground black
*   pepper*
1/8 tsp. garlic powder

1. In a covered jar, combine all ingredients.
2. Shake until well blended.

Yields 3/4 cup.

Vinaigrette

4 Tbsp. cider vinegar
1 tsp. dry mustard
2 Tbsp. olive oil

1/2 tsp. thyme
dash of freshly ground black
  pepper

1. In a small bowl, mix vinegar with mustard using a wire whisk.
2. Slowly add oil, whisking continuously.
3. Whisk in thyme and pepper.

Yields 1/2 cup

Salsa

2 medium tomatoes,
  chopped
1/2 cup chopped scallions
2 Tbsp. chopped
  jalapeno

1 Tbsp. red wine vinegar
2 tsp. olive oil
1/2 tsp. freshly ground black
  pepper

1. Combine all ingredients in a small bowl.
2. Chill for at least one hour before serving.

Yields 1 1/2 cups

Home-Style Tomato Sauce

2 tsp. olive oil
1 small onion, chopped
1/2 small green pepper,
  chopped
2 lb. tomatoes, peeled
1 1/2 tsp. garlic powder

1 1/2 tsp. oregano
1/4 tsp. freshly ground black
  pepper
1 cup sliced mushrooms
  (optional)

1. In a large skillet, heat oil; saute onion and green pepper until tender.

2. Add tomatoes and seasonings.
3. Bring to a boil Cover and let simmer for 30 to 45 minutes.

Yields 2 to 3 cups

Miscellaneous

Mock Sour Cream

> *1 cup low-fat cottage cheese*
>
> *1/2 cup low-fat yogurt*
> *2 Tbsp. lemon juice*

1. In a blender or food processor, combine all ingredients.
2. Blend until smooth. Chill before serving.

Yields 1 1/2 cups.

Egg Substitute

> *1/4 cup non-fat dried milk*
>
> *6 egg whites*
> *1 Tbsp. vegetable oil*

1. In a blender, combine all ingredients.
2. Blend until smooth. Freeze or store in a covered jar in the refrigerator for up to one week. Use as an egg substitute in baking or to make scrambled eggs and omelets.

Yields 1 cup

Whole Wheat Stuffing

4 slices stale whole
    wheat bread
1 small apple, cored and
    chopped
1/4 medium onion,
    chopped
1 stalk celery, chopped
1 Tbsp. raisins

2 egg whites, beaten
2 Tsp. diet margarine, melted
dash of freshly ground black
    pepper
1 tsp. chopped parsley
1/4-1/2 cup warm chicken
    broth

1. Cut bread into small cubes.
2. In a mixing bowl, combine bread cubes, apple, onion, celery and raisins.
3. Stir in egg and margarine, mixing to coat evenly.
4. Add enough broth to moisten.
5. Transfer into a small casserole dish. Bake at 350 degrees for 20 to 30 minutes or until browned and crisp on top.

Serves 2

Bulgur-Wheat Pilaf

2 tsp. olive oil
1 small carrot, diced
1 stalk celery, diced
1/3 cup sliced mushrooms

1 bay leaf
1 3/4 cup water
1 cup raw bulgar-wheat
dash of salt

1. In a heavy skillet, heat oil. Saute vegetables with bay leaf until tender.
2. Add water and bring to a boil; cover and let simmer for five minutes.
3. Stir in bulgar-wheat and season with salt. Bring to a boil.
4. Reduce heat, cover and let simmer for 15 minutes.

5. Uncover and continue to simmer until liquid is fully reduced.

Yields 4 cups

Cheese-Stuffed Potato

1 large baked potato
1 Tbsp. skim milk
1/4 cup part-skim ricotta cheese
dash of freshly ground black pepper

1 oz. part-skim mozzarella cheese, shredded
1 tsp. grated parmesan cheese

1. Slice top off the potato; discard top.
2. Use a melon baller to scoop out flesh.
3. Mash flesh with milk using a potato masher.
4. Stir in ricotta cheese, pepper and shredded mozzarella.
5. Stuff into hollowed potato skin. Sprinkle with grated parmesan cheese.
6. Bake at 350 degrees for 15 minutes or until heated through.

Serves 2

Whole Grain Corn Muffins

1/4 cup vegetable oil
1/4 cup honey
1 1/4 cup skim milk
1 egg, beaten
1 cup whole wheat flour

1/2 tsp. salt
1/4 cup wheat germ
4 tsp. baking powder
1 cup yellow cornmeal

1. In a mixing bowl, combine oil with honey. Add milk and egg, and mix well.
2. In a separate bowl, mix together flour, salt, wheat germ and baking powder.
3. Pour the liquid mixture into the dry ingredients, stirring briskly until just moistened.
4. Stir in cornmeal. Do not overmix!
5. Fill paper-lined muffin tins 2/3 full.
6. Bake at 425 degrees for 20 to 25 minutes, or until toothpick inserted in center comes clean.

Yields 12

EASY
SHOPPING
PLANNER

To ensure that you have on hand all of the foods you will need in order to follow the *30 Day Menu Plan*, and prepare the accompanying recipes, use the *Easy Shopping Planner* below. Try to shop only once a week -- and NEVER when you are hungry! Note that each of the four weeks in the planner is divided into two lists:

- Have On Hand
- Purchase If Needed

Each week before you shop, examine both lists carefully to identify the foods that you already have in stock, as well as those items that you will need to buy. Then mark the foods needed to be purchased, and indicate the amount of each; amounts should be determined individually, based on family size and needs.

Be sure to read food labels carefully to check for:
- unsalted and low-sodium items
- 100 percent whole grain breads and cereals
- fat-free and low-fat foods
- low-calorie and reduced calorie items

Check the ingredient list of prepared foods to identify items that are:
- sugar-free or low in sugar
- cholesterol-free (contains no animal products)
- high-fiber (whole-grain, unprocessed or contains other bran)

Be a cautious consumer! Many products offer health-related, diet-related claims that are misleading or downright false!

Week One

Have On Hand

Spice Rack:
_____ basil, dried
_____ chives, chopped
_____ cinnamon
_____ curry powder
_____ dill
_____ garlic powder
_____ marjoram
_____ mustard, dry
_____ nutmeg
_____ oregano
_____ onion powder
_____ parsley, dried
_____ pepper, red
_____ peppercorns, black
_____ pepper flakes, red
_____ salt
_____ sesame seeds
_____ tarragon
_____ vanilla extract

Miscellaneous:
_____ almonds, slivered
_____ baking powder
_____ club soda
_____ herbal teas
_____ honey
_____ lemon juice
_____ molasses
_____ Dijon mustard

_____ olive oil
_____ peanut oil
_____ vegetable oil

_____ vinegar
_____ water, spring
_____ wine, white, dry

Purchase If Needed

Fruit/Juices
_____ apples
_____ applesauce
_____ bananas
_____ blueberries
_____ cantaloupe
_____ dates
_____ grapes, seedless
_____ grapefruit
_____ grapefruit juice
_____ lemons
_____ nectarines
_____ oranges
_____ orange juice
_____ papaya
_____ peaches
_____ pears
_____ pineapple, crushed
_____ pineapple juice
_____ plums
_____ raisins
_____ strawberries

Vegetables
_____ bamboo shoots
_____ beans, green
_____ broccoli
_____ cabbage, red
_____ carrots, baby

_____ carrots
_____ celery
_____ eggplant
_____ garlic cloves
_____ garbanzo beans
_____ ginger
_____ green peppers
_____ mushrooms
_____ onions
_____ parsley
_____ pea pods
_____ potatoes, small, red
_____ radishes
_____ scallions
_____ spinach, fresh
_____ spinach, frozen,
    chopped
_____ tomatoes
_____ water chestnuts
_____ zucchini
    PLUS:
_____ raw vegetables,
    assorted salad
    ingredients, as
    desired

Breads/Cereals/Grain
_____ bran cereal
_____ bran, unprocessed

HEART WATCHERS DIET & MENU PLANNER

_____ bread, Italian
_____ bread, whole wheat
_____ bread sticks, whole wheat
_____ crackers, rye-crisp
_____ crackers, whole-grain
_____ English muffins, whole wheat
_____ Familia cereal
_____ flour, whole wheat
_____ ginger snaps
_____ graham crackers
_____ oats, rolled
_____ pita, whole wheat, small
_____ popcorn kernels
_____ rolls, whole-grain, small
_____ rice, brown
_____ spaghetti, whole wheat
_____ wheat germ

Milk/Dairy Products
_____ buttermilk, skimmed
_____ cheese, low-fat
_____ cheese, parmesan, grated
_____ cheese, part-skim mozzarella
_____ cottage cheese, low-fat
_____ eggs

_____ milk, skim
_____ yogurt, low-fat, lemon
_____ yogurt, low-fat, plain
_____ yogurt, low-fat, vanilla

Meat, Poultry, Fish
_____ chicken, boneless breasts
_____ fish, fresh, fillets
_____ fish, white, firm-fleshed
_____ ground beef, extra lean
_____ turkey, cooked
_____ shrimp, fresh or frozen

Add To Spice Rack
_____ sesame tabini
_____ soy sauce, low-sodium
_____ tamari

New Miscellaneous Items
_____ diet margarine
_____ diet mayonnaise
_____ peanut butter, old-fashioned/natural
_____ salad dressings, low-calorie
_____ tomato sauce, natural/light

Week Two

Have On Hand

_____

Breads/Cereals/Grain
_____ bran cereal
_____ bran, unprocessed
_____ Familia cereal
_____ flour, whole wheat
_____ oats, rolled
_____ popcorn kernels
_____ rice, brown
_____ wheat germ

Miscellaneous
_____ almonds, slivered
_____ club soda
_____ diet margarine
_____ diet mayonnaise

_____ herbal teas
_____ honey
_____ lemon juice
_____ mustard, Dijon-
         style
_____ olive oil
_____ peanut butter, old-
         fashioned/natural
_____ peanut oil
_____ salad dressings,
         low-calorie
_____ vegetable oil
_____ walnuts
_____ water, spring
_____ wine, white, dry

Purchase If Needed

Fruits/Juices
_____ apples
_____ applesauce
_____ bananas
_____ blueberries
_____ cantaloupe
_____ dates
_____ fresh fruit salad
_____ grapes, seedless
_____ grapefruit juice
_____ mango
_____ nectarines

_____ oranges
_____ orange juice
_____ peaches
_____ pears
_____ pineapple, crushed
_____ pineapple juice
_____ raisins
_____ strawberries

Vegetables
_____ asparagus
_____ avocados

87

HEART WATCHERS DIET & MENU PLANNER

_____ black beans
_____ cabbage, red
_____ carrots
_____ celery
_____ cucumbers
_____ eggplant
_____ garlic cloves
_____ kidney beans
_____ lettuce
_____ mint, fresh
_____ mushrooms
_____ onions
_____ parsley
_____ peppers, green
_____ peppers, jalapeno
_____ radishes
_____ scallions
_____ sprouts, alfalfa
_____ tomatoes
_____ tomato juice, low-
    sodium
_____ zucchini

Breads/Cereals/Grains
_____ bread, whole wheat
_____ bread crumbs,
    whole wheat
_____ bread sticks, whole
    wheat
_____ cornmeal, yellow
_____ corn tortillas, small
_____ crackers, whole-
    grain
_____ English muffins,
    whole wheat

_____ fig cookies
_____ pasta, whole wheat
    or vegetable shells
_____ rice, white
_____ rolls, whole-grain,
    small

Milk/Dairy Products
_____ buttermilk,
    skimmed
_____ cheese, low-fat
_____ cheese, parmesan,
    grated
_____ cheese, part-skim
    mozzarella
_____ cottage cheese,
    low-fat
_____ eggs
_____ milk, skim
_____ yogurt, low-fat,
    lemon
_____ yogurt, low-fat,
    plain
_____ yogurt, low-fat,
    vanilla

Meat, Poultry, Fish
_____ chicken, (or
    turkey), cooked
_____ ground beef, extra
    lean
_____ salmon, canned
_____ tuna, water-packed

Add To Spice Rack
_____ baking soda
_____ bay leaves
_____ cayenne pepper
_____ chili powder
_____ thyme

New Miscellaneous Items
_____ chicken broth, low-
    sodium
_____ confectioners'

    sugar
_____ Kirsch
_____ tomato paste, low-
    sodium
_____ tomato puree, low-
    sodium
_____ vinegar, red wine
_____ vinegar, white wine
_____ wine, red, dry

Week Three

Have On Hand

Breads/Cereals/Grain
_____ bran, unprocessed
_____ Familia cereal
_____ fig cookies
_____ flour, whole wheat
_____ oats, rolled
_____ popcorn, kernels
_____ rice, brown
_____ wheat germ

Miscellaneous
_____ almonds, slivered
_____ club soda
_____ chicken broth, low-
    sodium
_____ diet margarine
_____ diet mayonnaise
_____ herbal teas

_____ honey
_____ lemon juice
_____ mustard, Dijon-
    style
_____ olive oil
_____ peanut oil
_____ salad dressing, low-
    calorie
_____ tomato sauce,
    natural/light
_____ vegetable oil
_____ vinegar, red wine
_____ walnuts
_____ water, spring
_____ wine, red, dry
_____ wine, white, dry

Purchase If Needed

Fruits/Juices

_____ apples
_____ apple juice
_____ applesauce
_____ bananas
_____ blueberries
_____ cantaloupes
_____ dates
_____ figs
_____ fresh fruit salad
_____ grapes, seedless
_____ grapefruit
_____ grapefruit juice
_____ honeydew melon
_____ lemons
_____ limes
_____ nectarines
_____ oranges
_____ orange juice
_____ peaches
_____ pears
_____ pineapple, chunks
_____ pineapple, crushed
_____ pineapple juice
_____ raisins
_____ strawberries

Vegetables

_____ broccoli
_____ cabbage, red
_____ carrots
_____ celery
_____ cherry tomatoes
_____ corn-on-the-cob
_____ cucumbers
_____ garlic cloves
_____ lettuce
_____ mushrooms
_____ mushroom caps, large
_____ onions
_____ parsley
_____ peppers, green
_____ peppers, jalapeno
_____ potatoes, small baking
_____ radishes
_____ scallions
_____ spinach, fresh
_____ sprouts, alfalfa
_____ sweet potatoes
_____ tomatoes
_____ tomato juice, low-sodium
_____ zucchini

Breads/Cereals/Grain

_____ bread, Italian
_____ bread, whole wheat
_____ bread sticks, whole wheat
_____ crackers, whole-grain
_____ English muffins, whole wheat
_____ graham crackers

_____ pita, whole wheat, small

_____ rolls, whole-grain, small

_____ spaghetti, whole wheat

_____ wild rice

Milk/Dairy Products

_____ buttermilk, skimmed

_____ cheese, low-fat

_____ cheese, parmesan, grated

_____ cheese, part-skim mozzarella

_____ cottage cheese, low-fat

_____ eggs

_____ milk, skim

_____ yogurt, low-fat lemon

_____ yogurt, low-fat, plain

_____ yogurt, low-fat, vanilla

Meat, Poultry, Fish

_____ chicken, breasts, large

_____ chicken, boneless breasts

_____ chicken (or turkey), cooked

_____ fish, fresh, fillets

_____ scallops, bay

_____ tuna, water-packed

_____ turkey cutlets, boneless and skinless

Add To Spice Rack

_____ celery seed

_____ rosemary

Week Four

Have On Hand

Breads/Cereals/Grains

_____ bran cereal

_____ bran, unprocessed

_____ Familia cereal

_____ fig cookies

_____ graham crackers

_____ oats, rolled

_____ popcorn kernels

_____ rice, brown

_____ wheat germ

_____ wild rice

Miscellaneous
_____ almonds, slivered
_____ club soda
_____ chicken broth, low-sodium
_____ confectioners' sugar
_____ diet margarine
_____ diet mayonnaise
_____ herbal tea
_____ honey
_____ Kirsch
_____ lemon juice
_____ mustard, Dijon-style
_____ olive oil
_____ peanut butter, old-fashioned/natural
_____ peanut oil
_____ salad dressing, low-calorie, Italian
_____ tomato sauce, natural/light
_____ vinegar, red wine
_____ vinegar, white wine
_____ walnuts
_____ water, spring
_____ wine, red, dry
_____ wine, white, dry

Purchase If Needed

Fruits/Juices
_____ apples
_____ apple juice
_____ applesauce
_____ bananas
_____ blueberries
_____ cantaloupe
_____ dates
_____ fresh fruit salad
_____ grape juice
_____ grapefruit
_____ grapefruit juice
_____ lemons
_____ mango
_____ oranges
_____ orange juice
_____ orange juice, frozen con-centrate
_____ peaches
_____ pears
_____ pineapple, chunks
_____ pineapple, crushed
_____ pineapple, fresh rings
_____ pineapple juice
_____ plums
_____ raisins
_____ strawberries
_____ tangerines

Easy Shopping Planner

Vegetables

_____ asparagus
_____ avocados
_____ bamboo shoots
_____ beans. green
_____ black beans
_____ broccoli
_____ Brussels sprouts
_____ cabbage, red
_____ carrots
_____ cauliflower
_____ celery
_____ cherry tomatoes
_____ cucumbers
_____ eggplant
_____ garbanzo beans
   (canned)
_____ garlic cloves
_____ kale
_____ lettuce
_____ mint, fresh
_____ mushrooms,
   canned (whole),
   low-sodium
_____ onions
_____ parsley
_____ pea pods
_____ peppers, green
_____ peppers, red
_____ potatoes, small red
_____ potatoes, large
   baking
_____ radishes
_____ scallions

_____ spinach, fresh
_____ sprouts, alfalfa
_____ summer squash
_____ sweet potatoes
_____ tarragon, fresh
_____ tomatoes
_____ tomatoes, canned
   (whole), low-
   sodium
_____ water chestnuts
_____ zucchini

Breads/Cereals/Grains

_____ bagels, whole
   wheat (or
   pumpernickel)
_____ bread, whole wheat
_____ bread sticks, whole
   wheat
_____ bulgar-wheat, raw
_____ crackers, rye-crisp
_____ cornmeal
_____ corn tortillas, small
_____ English muffins,
   whole wheat
_____ Grape Nuts cereal
_____ pasta, whole wheat
   or vegetable shells
_____ pita, whole wheat,
   small
_____ rice, whole
_____ rolls, whole grain,
   small

HEART WATCHERS DIET & MENU PLANNER

Milk/Dairy Products

_____ buttermilk, skimmed

_____ cheese, low-fat

_____ cheese, parmesan grated

_____ cheese, part-skim mozzarella

_____ cheese, part-skim ricotta

_____ cottage cheese, low-fat

_____ eggs

_____ milk, skim

_____ yogurt, low-fat, lemon

_____ yogurt, low-fat, plain

_____ yogurt, low-fat, vanilla

Meats/Poultry/Fish

_____ chicken, boneless and skinless

_____ fish, fresh, fillets

_____ fish, white, firm-fleshed

_____ lamb, lean

_____ swordfish, fresh

_____ tuna, water-packed

_____ turkey, skinless

Add To Spice Rack

_____ cumin

_____ paprika

New Miscellaneous Items

_____ cranberry sauce, natural

DINING OUT
DO'S &
DON'TS

J ust because you are being careful in your food selections, you do not have to give up restaurants altogether, nor opt for brown bag lunches every day. By following a few basic rules, you can make wise food choices almost anywhere--whether at a fast food outlet, a gourmet banquet or a local cafeteria. In order to make menu selctions that are low in cholesterol, sodium and calories, keep in mind the following:

DO'S	DON'TS
Appetizers: fresh vegetables	bouillons or
fresh fruits	consommes
fruit salad,	soups or chowders
unsweetened	marinated vegetables
fresh fruit juice	salted crackers
seafood, steamed or	chips, dips, etc.
cocktails	nuts
	caviar

HEART WATCHERS DIET & MENU PLANNER

	DO'S	DON'TS

Salads:	green, tossed
	chef's with poultry
	spinach, no egg or
	  bacon
	low-calorie dressings
	oil and vinegar
	Note: request that
	* dressings be served*
	* on the side*
		mayonnaise-based
		  salads
		potato salad
		egg salad
		creamy coleslaw
		chef's with egg,
		  fatty meats
		spinach with egg,
		  bacon
		commercial salad

Vegetables:	any plain, fresh	buttered, canned,
		  creamed, fried,
		  marinated, pickled,
		  seasoned, sauced

Breads:	whole grain breads
	breadsticks,
	  unsalted
	French or Italian
	pita bread
	crackers, unsalted
	dinner rolls, plain
	English muffins
	bagels
		garlic bread
		egg or cheese breads
		hard rolls
		submarine rolls
		breadsticks, salted
		crackers, butter or
		  cheese
		crackers, salted
		biscuits
		croissants
		muffins
		butter rolls
		sweet rolls

Meat:	lean, trimmed cuts
	--baked, boiled
	broiled, roasted
	no gravies or sauces
		breaded, fried,
		  marinated cuts
		gravies, stews,
		  sauces

Dining Out Do's & Don'ts

	DO'S	DON'TS
Poultry:	chicken or turkey, skin removed-- baked, boiled, broiled, roasted no gravies or sauces	goose, duck breaded, fried, marinated cuts gravies, stews, sauces (cream, cheese, soy, tomato, white)
Fish and Shellfish:	any (prepared with minimal use of margarine)--baked, boiled, broiled, poached	breaded, fried, frozen fillets dried, pickled, smoked
Desserts:	angel food cake, frozen fruit ices, sorbets, fruits-- fresh, baked, dried, poached	rich sweets: cake candy, cookies, doughnuts, ice cream, pastries, puddings
Beverages:	fruit juices skim, lowfat milk coffee, tea light beers, dry wines	tomato juice, vegetable juice cocktails shakes, eggnog cream, cream substitutes sweetened alcoholic beverages and liqueurs

Extras:

lemon juice, herbs
spices
cottage cheese,
low-fat

pickles, relishes
mustard, ketchup,
cocktail sauce,
steak sauce
Worcestershire sauce
mayonnaise
sour cream
bacon bits

ADDITIONAL NOTE:

Read menus carefully to avoid selections described as:

- buttered, butter, butter sauce
- creamed, creamy, cream sauce
- fried, french fried, pan fried, crispy
- au gratin, cheese sauce, escalloped
- a la king, bernaise, hollandaise
- casserole, hash, pot pie, stew
- marinated, pickled, sauteed, smoked
- all you can eat

Remember, the key to successful dining out is to follow the *Heartwatchers' Diet Plan*. When this is impossible, choose your foods carefully and eat them in moderation. It may prove wiser **not** to do, that to **over**do!

PLANNING COUNTER

Breakfast Food Selections

Choose from the following **low calorie** foods to create your own delicious and nutritious breakfast menus. Note that all items contain no more than 150 calories per serving. Choose foods from the **protein food selections** section to further enhance your menu.

KEY:	Amt	= amount	dia	= diameter
	Pro	= protein	lb	= pound
	Cho	= carbohydrates	sm	= small
	Na	= sodium	med	= medium
	Chol	= cholesterol	mini	= miniature
	Cals	= calories	sl	= slice
	t	= trace amount	pkg	= package
	tsp	= teaspoon	sq	= square
	tbsp	= tablespoon	"	= inch
	oz	= ounce	cu. in.	= cubic inch

HEART WATCHERS DIET & MENU PLANNER

Food	Amt	Pro	Fat	Cho	Na	Chol	Cals
Applesauce:							
canned, unsweetened	1 cup	.5	.5	26.4	5	0	100
Apricots, canned							
unsweetened,	1 cup	1.7	.2	23.6	2	0	93
fresh halves	1 cup	1.6	.3	19.8	2	0	79
Banana, fresh							
7 3/4" long	1 cup	1.0	.2	21.1	1	0	81
Blackberries: fresh	1 cup	1.7	1.3	18.6	1	0	84
frozen,unsweetened	1 cup	1.1	.4	34.9	1	0	137
Blueberries: fresh	1 cup	1.0	.7	22.2	1	0	90
frozen,unsweetened	1 cup	1.2	.8	22.4	2	0	91
Cantaloupe:							
fresh: 5" dia.	1/2	1.9	.3	20.4	33	0	82
diced	1 cup	1.1	.2	12.0	19	0	48
Casaba melon:							
fresh, 7 3/4" long	1/10	1.7	t	9.1	17	0	38
Cereal:							
puffed rice	1 cup	.9	.1	13.4	t	0	60
puffed wheat	1 cup	2.3	.2	11.8	1	0	54
shredded wheat	1 bis.	2.5	.5	20.0	1	0	89
Wheat germ	1 tbs.	1.8	.7	3.0	t	0	23
Cocoa powder							
medium fat	1 tbs.	.9	1.0	2.8	t	0	14
Cranberries, fresh							
whole	1 cup	.4	.7	10.3	2	0	44
Cream substitute,							
non-dairy	1 tbs.	.2	1.5	1.7	12	0	20
Fruit salad,							
canned,unsweetened	1 cup	1.0	.2	22.3	2	0	86
Grapefruit: canned,							
unsweetened	1 cup	1.5	.2	18.5	10	0	73
fresh, 3 9/16" dia.	1/2	.5	.1	10.3	1	0	40
fresh,sections	1 cup	1.0	.2	21.2	2	0	82
Guava, fresh	1 med.	2.0	t	11.7	3	0	48
Margarine, reg.	1 pat	t	4.1	t	49	0	36
Milk, skim	1 cup	8.4	.4	11.9	126	4	86

Food	Amt	Pro	Fat	Cho	Na	Chol	Cals
Nectarines, fresh							
2 1/2" dia.	1	.8	t	23.9	8	0	88
Oranges, fresh							
naval, 2 7/8" dia.	1	1.8	.1	17.8	1	0	71
sections	1 cup	1.8	.4	22.0	2	0	88
Bread: cracked wheat	1 sl.	2.2	.6	13.0	132	t	66
French (2 1/2" x 2							
x 1/2")	1 sl.	1.4	.5	8.3	87	t	44
raisin	1 sl.	1.7	.7	13.4	91	t	66
rye	1 sl.	2.3	.3	13.0	139	t	61
whole wheat	1 sl.	2.6	.7	13.8	148	t	67
Papaya, fresh,cubed	1 cup	.8	.1	14.0	4	0	55
Peanut butter,comrcl	1 tbs.	4.0	8.1	3.0	97	t	94
Pineapple, canned							
unsweetened, cuts							
(chunk,tidbit,crushed)	1 cup	.7	.2	25.1	2	0	96
Prunes, dried,large	1	.2	t	5.7	t	0	22
Raisins, seedless,							
whole	1 tbs.	.2	t	7.0	2	0	26
Rasberries, fresh							
black	1 cup	2.0	1.9	21.0	1	0	98
red	1 cup	1.5	.6	16.7	1	0	70
Strawberries, fresh							
whole	1 cup	1.0	.7	12.5	1	0	55
Tangelo, fresh							
2 3/4" dia.	1	.6	.1	11.1	2	0	47
Tangerine, fresh							
2 1/2" dia.	1	.8	.2	11.7	2	0	46
sections	1 cup	1.6	.4	22.6	4	0	90

Lunch and Dinner Food Selections

Choose from the following **low calorie** foods to create your own delicious and nutritious lunch and dinner menus. Note that all items contain no more than 150 calories per serving. Choose foods from the **protein food selections** section to further enhance your menus.

Food	Amt	Pro	Fat	Cho	Na	Chol	Cals
Artichokes: French or Globe, cooked	1 bud	3.4	.2	1	36	0	16
Jerusalem, pared, cooked	4 oz.	t	.2	18.9	2	0	75
Asparagus, fresh, spears, cooked	1 cup	4.0	.4	6.5	2	0	36
Bamboo shoots, fresh	1 cup	3.9	.5	7.9	1	0	41
Beans: green or snap, fresh, cooked	1 cup	2.0	.3	6.8	5	0	31
French style, frozen, cooked	1 cup	2.1	.1	7.8	3	0	34
sprouts, mung	1 cup	4.0	.2	6.9	5	0	37
Yellow or wax, frozen, cooked	1 cup	2.3	.1	8.4	1	0	36
Beets, fresh, diced or sliced	1 cup	1.9	.2	12.2	73	0	54
Beet greens, cooked	1 cup	2.5	.3	4.8	110	0	26
Boston brown bread, canned, 1/2" thick	1 sl.	2.5	.6	20.5	113	0	95

Food	Amt	Pro	Fat	Cho	Na	Chol	Cals
Bread: cracked wheat	1 sl.	2.2	.6	13.0	132	t	66
French (2 1/2" x 2" x 1/2")	1 sl.	1.4	.5	8.3	87	t	44
raisin	1 sl.	1.7	.7	13.4	91	t	66
rye	1 sl.	2.3	.3	13.0	139	t	61
whole wheat	1 sl.	2.6	.7	13.8	148	t	67
Breadsticks, 4 1/2"	1	1.2	.3	7.5	70	t	38
Broccli: fresh,stalks	1 med.	5.6	.5	8.1	18	0	47
frozen, chopped, cooked	1 cup	5.4	.6	8.5	28	0	48
Brussels sprouts, frozen, cooked	1 cup	5.0	.3	10.1	22	0	51
red, chopped	1 cup	1.8	.2	6.2	23	0	28
Cabbaage: white, wedges, cooked	1 cup	1.7	.3	6.8	22	0	31
Cake, from mix angel food, cubed	1 cu. in	.1	t	1.4	3	0	6
cupcake, uniced 2 1/2"	1	1.2	3.0	14.0	113	10	88
Carrots: fresh 7"	1	.8	.1	7.0	34	0	30
fresh,sliced,cooked	1 cup	1.4	.3	11.0	51	0	48
Cauliflower, fresh whole buds	1 cup	2.7	.2	5.2	13	0	27
frozen, cooked	1 cup	3.4	.4	5.9	18	0	32
Celery, fresh 8"	1 stalk	.4	t	1.6	50	0	7
Chard, Swiss, fresh, cooked	1 cup	2.6	.3	4.8	125	0	26
Cheese straws, 5"	1	.7	1.8	2.1	43	2	27
Cherries, sour fresh, whole-pitted	1 cup	1.9	.5	22.2	3	0	90
Collards: fresh,cooked	1 cup	6.8	1.3	9.7	40	0	63
frozen, chopped, cooked	1 cup	4.9	.7	9.5	27	0	51

HEART WATCHERS DIET & MENU PLANNER

Food	Amt	Pro	Fat	Cho	Na	Chol	Cals
Cookes: butter thins 2" dia.	1	.3	.9	3.6	21		323
graham crackers, plain	2" sq.	.6	.7	5.2	48	t	28
Corn, fresh, on the cob, cooked	5" ear	2.5	.8	16.2	t	0	70
Crackers, butter, round, 1 7/8" dia.	1	.2	.6	2.2	36	t	15
rye wafers, 3 1/2" x 1 7/8"	1	.9	t	5.0	57	0	22
soda, 1 7/8" sq.	1	.3	.4	2.0	31	0	12
soda, biscuit, 2 3/8" x 2 1/8"	1	.5	.7	3.6	55	0	22
Pineapple: canned, unsweetend, cuts-chunks, crushed, tidbits	1 cup	.7	.2	25.1	2	0	96
fresh, sliced 3 1/2" dia.	1	.3	.2	11.5	1	0	44
Plums, fresh: Damson, 1" dia.	10	.5	t	17.8	2	0	66
Japanese, diced	1 cup	.8	.3	20.3	2	0	79
Prune type, 1 1/2"	1	.2	.1	5.6	t	0	21
Raisins, seedless, whole	1 tbs.	.2	t	7.0	2	0	26
Rhubarb, fresh, diced	1 cup	.7	.1	4.5	2	0	20
Rutabagas, fresh, cooked, mashed	1 cup	2.2	.2	19.7	10	0	84
Salad dressings, commercial: French, low-cal	1 tbs.	.1	.7	2.5	126	0	15
Italian,low-cal	1 tbs.	.7	.4	.4	t	0	8
Russian,low-cal	1 tbs.	.1	.7	4.5	26	1	23
mayonnaise type	1 tbs.	.2	6.3	2.2	88	4	65
low-calorie	1 tbs.	.2	2.0	.8	19	t	22

Planning Counter

Food	Amt	Pro	Fat	Cho	Na	Chol	Cals
Thousand island low-cal	1 tbs.	.1	2.1	2.3	105	2	27
Soybean curd (tofu) 2 1/2" x 2 3/4"	1 pce	9.4	5.0	2.9	8	0	86
sprouts	1 cup	6.5	1.5	5.6	3	0	48
Spinach, fresh, chopped	1 cup	1.8	.2	2.4	39	0	14
frozen,leaf,cooked	1 cup	5.5	.6	7.4	93	0	46
Squash, summer, fresh,cooked,sliced	1 cup	1.3	.2	6.8	2	0	29
Squash, winter, fresh: acorn, baked 4" dia.	1/2	3.0	.2	21.8	2	0	86
butternut, boiled, mashed	1 cup	2.7	.2	25.5	2	0	100
hubbard, boiled, diced	1 cup	2.6	.7	16.2	2	0	71
Tomatoes: fresh 2 3/5" dia.	1	1.4	.2	5.8	4	0	27
fresh,cooked	1 cup	3.1	.5	13.3	10	0	63
Turnip, cooked, mashed	1 cup	1.8	.5	11.3	78	0	53
Turnip greens, frozen,chopped, cooked	1 cup	4.1	.5	6.4	28	0	38
Water chestnuts, Chinese	1 oz.	.3	6	4.2	4	0	17
Watercress, fresh chopped	1 cup	2.3	.4	3.8	65	0	24
Watermelon, fresh, diced	1 cup	.8	.3	10.2	2	0	42

Snack Selections

Choose from the following **low calorie** foods to create your own delicious and nutritious snacks. Note all items contain no more than 150 calories per serving. Choose from the **protein food selections** section to further enhance your snacks.

Food	Amt	Pro	Fat	Cho	Na	Chol	Cals
Apples, fresh whole, 3" dia.	1	.3	1.0	24.0	2	0	96
Applesauce, canned, unsweetened	1 cup	.5	.5	26.4	5	0	100
Apricots, fresh, whole	3	1.1	.2	13.7	1	0	55
Banana, fresh 7 3/4" long	1 cup	1.0	.2	21.1	1	0	81
Blackberries, fresh	1 cup	1.7	1.3	18.6	1	0	84
Blueberries, fresh	1 cup	1.0	.7	22.2	1	0	90
Breadsticks, 4 1/2"	1	1.2	.3	7.5	70	t	38
Cake, from mix angel food, cubed	1" cube	.1	t	1.4	3	0	6
Celery, fresh 8" long	1 stalk	.4	t	1.6	50	0	7
Cherries, sour, fresh whole (pitted)	1 cup	1.9	.5	22.2	3	0	90
Crackers: butter, round, 1 7/8" dia.	1	.2	.6	2.2	36	t	15
rye wafers, 3 1/2" x 1 7/8")	1	.9	t	5.0	57	0	22
soda, 1 7/8" sq.	1	.3	.4	2.0	31	0	12

Planning Counter

Food	Amt	Pro	Fat	Cho	Na	Chol	Cals
soda,biscuit, (2 3/8" x 2 1/8")	1	.5	.7	3.6	55	0	22
wheat thins	4	2.0	3.1	4.8	23	t	55
zwieback, 3 1/2" x 1 1/2"	1	.7	.6	5.2	18	t	30
Fig: dried	1	.6	.2	14.5	7	0	55
fresh, 2 1/4" dia	1	.6	.2	10.2	1	0	40
Gooseberries, fresh	1 cup	1.2	.3	14.6	2	0	59
Granadilla (passion fruit) fresh	1	.4	.1	3.9	5	0	16
Grapefruit, fresh 3 9/16" dia.	1/2	.5	.1	10.3	1	0	40
Grapes, fresh, American-type	1 cup	1.3	1.0	15.9	3	0	70
Guava, fresh	1 med.	2.0	t	11.7	3	0	48
Kumquat, fresh	1 sm.	t	t	3.4	5	0	15
Loganberries, fresh	1 cup	1.4	.9	21.5	1	0	89
Lychees, fresh	10	.8	.3	14.8	3	0	58
Margarine, reg.	1 pat	t	4.1	t	49	0	36
Nectarines, fresh 2 1/2" dia.	1	.8	t	23.6	8	0	88
Oranges, fresh, navel, 2 7/8" dia	1	1.8	.1	17.8	1	0	71
Papaya, fresh, cubed	1 cup	.8	.1	14.0	4	0	55
Peaches, fresh 2 1/2" dia.	1	.6	.1	9.7	1	0	38
diced	1 cup	1.1	.2	17.9	2	0	70
Peanut butter, commercial	1 tbs.	4.0	8.1	3.0	97	t	94
Pears, fresh: Bartlett, 2 1/2"	1	1.1	.7	25.1	3	0	100
Bosc, 2 1/2"	1	1.0	.6	21.6	3	0	86
Peppers, sweet: green, 3" dia.	1 ring	.1	t	.5	1	0	2
red, 3" dia.	1 ring	.1	t	.7	t	0	3

Food	Amt	Pro	Fat	Cho	Na	Chol	Cals
Pickles, sweet:							
chopped	1 tbs.	.1	t	3.6	69	0	15
gherkin midget	1	t	t	2.2	48	0	9
mustard (chow-chow)	1 tbs.	.2	.1	4.2	81	0	18
Pineapple: canned, unsweetended cuts-chunks,crushed,							
tidbits	1 cup	.7	.2	25.1	2	0	96
fresh, sliced,							
3 1/2" dia.	1	.3	.2	11.5	1	0	44
Plums, fresh:							
Damson, 1" dia.	10	.5	t	17.8	2	0	66
Japanese, 2 1/8"	1	.3	.1	8.1	1	0	32
Plum-type, 1 1/2"	1	.2	.1	5.6	t	0	21
Pomegranate, fresh							
3 3/8" dia.	1	.8	.5	25.3	5	0	97
Popcorn, plain	1 cup	.8	.3	4.6	t	0	23
Prunes, dried,large	1	.2	t	5.7	t	0	22
Radishes, fresh,							
large	10	.8	.1	2.9	15	0	14
Raisins, seedless,							
whole	1 tbs.	.2	t	7.0	2	0	26
Raspberries, fresh							
black	1 cup	2.0	1.9	21.0	1	0	98
red	1 cup	1.5	.6	16.7	1	0	70
Rusk, 3 3/8"	1	1.2	.8	6.4	22	t	38
Strawberries, fresh,							
whole	1 cup	1.0	.7	12.5	1	0	55
Tangelo, fresh 2 3/4"	1	.6	.1	11.1	2	0	47
Tangerine, fresh							
2 1/2"	1	.8	.2	11.7	2	0	46

Beverage Selections

Choose from the following **low-calorie** beverages at meals or snacks. Note that all items contain no more than 120 calories per serving.

Food	Amt	Pro	Fat	Cho	Na	Chol	Cals
Apple juice, canned or bottled	1 cup	.2	t	29.5	2	0	118
Beverages, alcoholic beer, light	12 oz.	t	t	3.0	-	0	96
wine, table (12% alcohol)	3 1/2 oz.	.1	0	4.3	5	0	87
Beverages, carbonated: club soda, unsweetened	12 oz.	0	0	0	39	0	0
tonic water	12 oz.	0	0	29.3	19	0	113
Cocoa: beverage pwdr	1 oz.	1.1	.6	25.3	76	0	98
medium-fat powder	1 tbs.	.9	1.0	2.8	t	0	2
Coffee, prepared, plain	1 cup	t	t	t	2	0	2
Grapefruit juice: canned, unsweetened	1 cup	1.2	.2	24.2	2	0	101
fresh	1 cup	1.2	.2	22.6	2	0	96
Grapefruit-orange juice, canned, unsweetened	1 cup	1.5	.5	24.9	2	0	106
Lemonade, frozen, sweetened	1 cup	.1	t	28.3	1	0	107

Food	Amt	Pro	Fat	Cho	Na	Chol	Cals
Limeade, frozen,							
sweetened	1 cup	.1	t	27.0	t	0	102
Milk: low-fat 2%	1 cup	8.1	4.7	11.7	122	18	121
skim	1 cup	8.4	.4	11.9	126	4	86
Orange juice:							
fresh	1 cup	1.7	.5	25.8	2	0	112
frozen,unsweetened	1 cup	2.0	.7	25.5	2	0	114
Tangelo juice, fresh	1 cup	1.2	.2	24.0	2	0	101
Tangerine juice:							
canned, unsweetened	1 cup	1.2	.5	24.9	2	0	106
fresh	1 cup	1.2	.5	26.8	2	0	114

Protein Food Selections

Choose from the following **low calorie** protein foods to enhance your meals and snacks. Note that all items contain no more than 200 calories per serving. In moderate amounts, these nutritious foods provide ample protein without contributing excessive amounts of calories.

Food	Amt	Pro	Fat	Cho	Na	Chol	Cals
Cottage cheese,							
uncreamed	1 cup	25.0	.6	2.7	19	10	123
Milk: lowfat 2%	1 cup	8.1	4.7	11.7	122	18	121
skim	1 cup	8.4	.4	11.9	126	4	86
Sardines, Atlantic							
canned, 3" long	1	2.9	1.3	t	99	25	24
Sausage, pork							
fresh, cooked	1 link	2.4	5.7	t	125	10	62

Food	Amt	Pro	Fat	Cho	Na	Chol	Cals
Yogurt, from lowfat milk, plain	8 oz.	11.9	3.5	16.0	159	14	144

Lunch & Dinner Selections

Food	Amt	Pro	Fat	Cho	Na	Chol	Cals
Beef, lean, trimmed, cooked:							
chuck, roast or steak	3 oz.	25.9	6.0	0	45	77	164
flank steak (London Broil)	3 oz.	25.9	6.2	0	45	77	167
ground, 10% fat	3 oz.	25.3	9.6	0	57	77	186
round steak	3 oz.	23.3	5.2	0	65	77	161
rump roast	3 oz.	24.7	7.9	0	61	77	177
sirloin, double-bone	3 oz.	26.0	8.1	0	64	77	184
sirloin, wedge- & round-bone	3 oz.	27.4	6.5	0	67	77	176
Bluefish, fresh baked w/ margarine	4 oz.	29.7	5.9	0	118	63	185
Cheese:							
Brie	1 oz.	5.9	7.9	.1	178	28	95
Brick	1 oz.	6.6	8.4	.8	159	27	105
Cheddar, domestic	1 oz.	7.1	9.4	.4	176	30	114
Colby	1 oz.	6.7	9.1	.7	171	27	112
Cottage, uncreamed	1 cup	25.0	.6	2.7	19	10	123
Mozzarella, part-skim	1 oz.	6.9	4.5	.8	132	16	72
Muenster	1 oz.	6.6	8.5	.3	178	27	104
Neufchatel	1 oz.	2.8	6.6	.8	113	22	74
Parmesan, grated	1 tbs.	2.1	1.5	.2	93	4	23
Swiss, domestic	1 oz.	8.1	7.8	1.0	74	26	107
Chicken:							
broiler	3 oz.	20.2	3.2	0	56	69	116
roaster	3 oz.	24.9	5.5	0	75	69	156

HEART WATCHERS DIET & MENU PLANNER

Food	Amt	Pro	Fat	Cho	Na	Chol	Cals
Cod, fresh, broiled							
with margarine	4 oz.	32.4	6.0	0	124	65	192
Goose, domesticated,							
cooked	3 oz.	28.8	8.3	0	105	36	198
Haddock, fresh							
oven-fried	4 oz.	22.4	7.2	6.4	200	77	188
Ham:							
boiled	1 oz.	5.4	4.8	0	49	70	66
deviled, canned	1 tbs.	1.8	4.2	0	122	15	46
fresh	3 oz.	25.2	8.5	0	62	80	184
fresh shoulder							
pork (picnic)	3 oz.	24.7	8.3	0	43	75	180
Halibut, fresh							
broiled with							
margarine	4 oz.	28.4	8.0	0	152	77	192
Rockfish, fresh							
cooked	4 oz.	20.4	2.8	2.0	96	65	120
Sardines, Atlantic							
canned, 3" long	1	2.9	1.3	t	99	25	24
Smelt, fresh	7 med.	-	-	0	30	77	100
Sole, fresh, cooked	4 oz.	-	-	0	89	77	90
Swordfish, fresh,							
broiled with							
margarine	4 oz.	29.6	6.4	0	-	77	184
Tongue, beef, cooked	2 oz.	12.2	9.5	.2	35	66	138
Tuna:							
canned in water	4 oz.	31.2	.9	0	46	72	144
fresh, cooked	3 oz.	-	-	0	46	60	105
Turkey, cooked							
light meat	3 oz.	28.0	3.3	0	70	65	150

Snack Selections:

Food	Amt	Pro	Fat	Cho	Na	Chol	Cals
Almonds, dried, shelled, chopped	1 tbs.	1.5	4.3	1.6	t	0	48
Brazil, nuts, shelled, large	6	4.1	19.0	3.1	t	0	185
Cheese (see Luncheon and Dinner Selections above)							
Cheese straws, 5"	1	.7	1.8	2.1	43	2	27
Chestnuts, in shell	10	2.1	1.1	30.7	4	0	141
Filberts	10	1.7	8.6	2.3	t	0	87
Ham, boiled	1 oz.	5.4	4.8	0	49	70	66
Ice milk, plain 5% fat	1 cup	5.2	5.6	29.1	105	18	184
Pecans, shelled, chopped	1 tbs.	.7	5.3	1.1	t	0	52
Sardines, Atlantic canned, 3" long	1	2.9	1.3	t	99	25	24
Walnuts, shelled, chopped	1 tbs.	1.2	5.1	1.3	t	0	52
Yogurt, from lowfat milk, plain	8 oz.	11.9	3.5	16.0	159	14	144

APPENDIX I. COMMON MEASUREMENTS CONVERSION TABLE

Use the table below to assist you in converting given quantities of foods into the desired equivalents.

5 milliliters	=	1 teaspoon
3 teaspoons	=	1 tablespoon
16 tablespoons	=	1 cup = 8 fluid ounces
2 cups	=	1 pint = 16 fluid ounces
2 pints	=	1 quart = 32 fluid ounces
4 quarts	=	1 gallon = 128 fluid ounces
28.35 grams	=	1 ounce = 2 fluid tablespoons
16 ounces	=	1 pound = 453.6 grams
8 quarts	=	1 peck
4 pecks	=	1 bushel

APPENDIX II. METRIC CONVERSION TABLE

The U.S. Department of Agriculture uses the following rounded figures for converting quantities of foods, energy values, and temperatures into metric system equivalents.

U.S. SYSTEM	Metric System Equivalent
Length:	
1 inch	2.54 centimeters,
	25.4 millimeters
Volume:	
1 cubic inch	16.39 cubic centimeters
1 teaspoon	5 milliliters
1 tablespoon	15 milliliters
1 fluid ounce	30 milliliters
1 cup	240 milliliters
1 pint	475 milliliters
1 quart	950 milliliters
1 gallon	3.8 liters
Energy:	
1 kilocalorie	4.184 kiloJoules
Temperature:	
1° Fahrenheit (F)	5/9° Celcius (C)

APPENDIX III. DESIRED WEIGHTS
(without clothing)

Prepared by the Metropolitan Life Insurance Company. Derived primarily from data of the Build and Blood Pressure Study, 1959, Society of Actuaries.

Height (Without Shoes)	Small Frame	Medium Frame	Large Frame
Women			
5 ft. 0 in.	92-98	96-107	104-109
5 ft. 1 in.	94-101	98-110	106-112
5 ft. 2 in.	96-104	101-112	109-118
5 ft. 3 in.	99-107	104-116	112-121
5 ft. 4 in.	102-110	107-119	115-125
5 ft. 5 in.	105-113	110-122	118-130
5 ft. 6 in.	108-116	113-126	121-135
5 ft. 7 in.	111-119	116-130	125-140
5 ft. 8 in.	114-123	120-135	129-145
5 ft. 9 in.	118-127	124-139	133-150
5 ft. 10 in.	122-131	128-143	137-155
5 ft. 11 in.	126-135	132-147	141-160
6 ft. 0 in.	130-140	136-151	145-165
Men			
5 ft. 4 in.	115-123	121-131	129-135
5 ft. 5 in.	118-126	124-136	132-137
5 ft. 6 in.	121-129	127-139	135-142
5 ft. 7 in.	124-133	130-143	138-148
5 ft. 8 in.	128-137	134-147	142-152
5 ft. 9 in.	132-141	138-152	147-155
5 ft. 10 in.	136-145	142-156	151-160
5 ft. 11 in.	140-150	146-160	155-165
6 ft. 0 in.	144-154	150-165	159-170
6 ft. 1 in.	148-158	154-170	164-175
6 ft. 2 in.	152-162	158-175	168-180
6 ft. 3 in.	156-167	162-180	173-185
6 ft. 4 in.	160-171	167-185	178-190